Easy First Food

Make this change enjoyable for your child and you

CAMILLA CONTI

HEALTH HARMONY

An imprint of
B. Jain Publishers (P) Ltd.
USA - EUROPE - INDIA

EASY FIRST FOOD

First Edition: 2011

1st Impression: 2011

All rights reserved. No part of this book may be reproduced, stored in a retrieval system or transmitted, in any form or by any means, mechanical, photocopying, recording or otherwise, without any prior written permission of the publisher.

© with the author

Published by Kuldeep Jain for

HEALTH  HARMONY

An imprint of

B. JAIN PUBLISHERS (P) LTD.

1921/10, Chuna Mandi, Paharganj, New Delhi 110 055 (INDIA)

Tel.: 91-11-4567 1000 • Fax: 91-11-4567 1010

Email: info@bjain.com • Website: **www.bjain.com**

Designed by: Anil Kumar

Printed in India by
J.J. OFFSET PRINTERS

ISBN: 978-81-319-1157-0

Dedication

To my grandmothers, Rina and Ines, who used to feed me beautiful food garnished with wonderful stories.

Alle mie nonne, Rina e Ines, che mi nutrivano di cibo buonissimo condito da storie fantastiche.

Acknowledgement

I would like to thank all the people who gave me the beautiful pictures incorporated in this book, my father Ezio, Elena and Karen, and all the mothers of the kids, La Leche League Italia.

A special thanks to my father and Franca who spent a whole week trying the various recipes contained in this book with me and photographing some of them. I thank my aunt Isa and my cousin Irene for cooking the 'vegetarian paella' and sharing their recipe with me.

Thanks to all the family members who supported me by taking care of my children while I was writing this book. I also thank my kids (especially the elder one!) for their cooperation.

Last but not the least, I thank Dr Gianfranco Trapani as I learnt a lot from him regarding nutrition.

Introduction

Once upon a time, there was a young boy who used to work in a rich man's house. The rich man was very strict with the boy and very greedy. The boy used to work hard the whole day and the only meal he would get was a slice of hard cheese.

Since he was not allowed to eat inside the house, the poor fellow would sit out on the stairs, facing the big orchard owned by the rich man. In the orchard, there were small plants and big trees.

When the season came, some of these trees started carrying big red and green coloured pears.

The pears were so ripe and inviting that one day the young boy, whose stomach was grumbling with hunger, could not resist. He won the fear of his greedy employer and he picked up one to eat it with his slice of cheese.

The boy found a hidden spot in the orchard and he started consuming his meals there. One bite to the cheese and one to the pear. The cheese had a strong milky and salty taste. The pear was sweet and juicy.

He immediately liked the combination. He gave a second bite to the cheese and then again the pear and he went on and on until both were over.

From that day onwards, for the whole season, he kept eating sweet juicy pears, along with his meager slice of cheese. The taste was so good that even the poor boy's hunger seemed to be a bit satiated by the sweetness of the fruit.

And, after every meal, the fellow used to repeat to himself: "May the owner never know, how tasty is the meal I owe!"

This is one of the many stories my grannies used to tell me when I was a kid, consuming my own slice of cheese accompanied by a sweet juicy pear and figuring out that yes, it was so tasty indeed!

Simple, natural and local food can be very pleasant for children, if they are fed with love and accompanied to explore real tastes from the very beginning.

This book is an invitation to be simple, to help your children discover the tastes and smells of your culture and geographic area, with patience and common sense.

I am convinced that, except a few things (avoiding junk food, respecting the child's rhythms and preferences, being careful towards allergenic foods), there are no life recipes or other prescriptions that can be given to a mother regarding her child's diet.

Children from different cultures have been growing up very well in every region of the world – and the diets are so different from each other! An Eskimo's baby might be given whale's fat, an Indian child lentils and an Italian parmesan, while the Chinese might have pork's tongue as first solid food. No matter what, they all grow and they are all fine and healthy.

A research work that I conducted sometime back about weaning in different cultures brought me to this conclusion - we fuss and worry so much about our children's food but in fact the truth is that there is nothing to worry about. Everything and its contrary is true, provided we avoid industrial processed foods and choose natural, local and seasonal stuff. The only little suggestion that I would give is to avoid or postpone the introduction of certain foods if any family member is allergic to those. And, most of all, to introduce solids only and only when the child is ready for this step.

All the rest is up to the child and the mother. This book is meant to give mothers and other caretakers a general know-how on the first solid foods and how to introduce them, without being prescriptive or imposing fixed meals and schedules. What I wish is to help you understand how to be in harmony with your child, how to recognize, read and respect his signals and clues. And especially how to make the introduction of solids an enjoyable adventure for both of you.

I will refer to the baby or child as a 'he' just for simplicity, since we will be mostly talking about children and mothers, and the mother is definitely a 'she'. I will call the child 'he' to avoid confusion.

With my best wishes for enjoying this new experience,

Camilla Conti

Publisher's Note

We are very proud to come out with the second book in this series titled "Easy". This series focuses on parenting issues for early childhood. This book is for level 2 where the child has to start solid foods after his intake of milk for all these months. It's an obvious change but can be stressful for the child and the parents many times. The idea of this book is to help the parents take the right decisions about various doubts which come to their mind during this phase.

The is not a jargon in what to give and what not to give as each and every continent has a different diet and food habits. The book will help you choose what is best for your child and his/her needs. The book will guide the parents how to understand their child's needs and preferences.

It's important for the child to develop an interest in eating and enjoy the same. The book will help you do that. At the same time it guides you as to how to plan a balanced diet keeping the child's taste and preferences in mind.

There is a section on how to develop the bond between you and your child and teach your child so many things about food at the same time. At the end there is a section on recipes which are healthy and tasty and has ingredients that are used world over.

We hope you enjoy this book and use this book to develop good eating habits and lay the foundation of health and fitness for your child ahead.

Kuldeep Jain
C.E.O., B.Jain Publishers (P) Ltd.

Foreword

I am glad to review this work by Camilla Conti which I feel is a very practical tool for all mothers of today. Here the child is placed at the center of his/her experience of starting solids. Lots of emphasis is put on the idea of respecting the child's stage of readiness and timings to start a new food experience. These phases are presented in a way, which is easy to tailor on individual child's needs and are not indicated as prescriptive time frames.

Introduction of solid food is part of a natural process, which ideally starts with breastfeeding and goes on in harmony between mother and child. The playful method for the introduction of solids is presented as a joyful path of discovery that mother and child can walk together at their own pace, making their own choices - i.e. what is good for them, not simply what is good generally.

Children must never be forced to eat against their appetite. Emphasis is put on the fact that children should be allowed to explore the food, to manipulate it and form their own relationship with it. Regarding this point, realistic growth parameters as suggested by WHO are provided.

The basic concept behind the whole book is that there are huge variations in children diets from one area of the world to the other. Given few basic general principles (e.g. mind allergenic foods, especially in case someone from the family suffers from allergy) most traditional diets are fine, although different from each other.

In the present scenario, mothers are caught between two equally disruptive fires: dogmas and prescriptions from grandparents, pediatricians and other child specialists on one side, the force of market advertisements on the other side. So mothers tend to give up their own wisdom and instinct to follow the directions of these powerful "authorities".

The book gives guidance and suggestions to mothers. The major strength points of this book are, firstly it includes suggestions for healthy, natural and local ingredients, no junks, simply because we are talking about kids. Secondly, it is not prescriptive or excessively didactic, on the contrary it aims at empowering parents to relax and trust themselves and their kids to clues and preferences in feeding them.

Dr. (Mrs.) B. Arora
B.Sc. (Gold Medalist), M.Sc., Ph.D. Nutrition
(University of Leeds, U.K.)
Ex. Assoc. Prof. (Nutrition P.A.U., Ludhiana)
Founder Director Shemrock Group of Schools
Delhi's No. 1 Preschool Chain

Contents

Dedication	iii
Acknowledgement	v
Introduction	vii
Publisher's Note	xi
Foreword	xiii

PART I – A BIT OF KNOW-HOW

THE FIRST COMPLEMENTARY FOODS — 1-7
    Is your baby ready to start? — 3
    Complementation vs substitution — 5

A CHILD CENTERED MEAL — 8-21
    Learn to respect your child's appetite — 9
    Never force him to eat — 10
    Do not rush — 11
    Let him mess up a bit — 12
    Respect his preferences — 14
    Go healthy, no junks — 15
    Chart 1 Cooking methods — 17
    Relax and take care of the environment — 19
    Do not leave him alone — 20
    Not only food, they need to grow healthy — 20
    Chart 2 A note on baby foods — 21

HERE WE GO! — 22-39
    Overview on nutrients — 23
    Carbohydrates — 23
    Proteins — 24
    Vitamins and minerals — 24

Fats	25
Chart 3 The food pyramid	25
Foods know-how	26
The very first bites	27
Beginnings	28
Later	30
Condiments	35
Beverages	36
Veg or non-veg?	36
How much do children really need?	37
GROWTH	**40-55**
Chart 4 WHO percentile growth charts	41
Foods for Growth	42
Fruits	44
Vegetables	47
Cereals	48
Pulses	50
Eggs	51
Dairy Products	51
Fish	52
Nuts	52
Condiments	53
Herbs and Spices	54
INTO TODDLERHOOD AND FURTHER	**56-61**
Learning and fun with food	56
Going for grocery with your child	56
Cooking with your child	57
Decorating dishes	58
Inventing recipes	58
Playing the restaurant game	58

Going for picnics	58
A small kitchen garden	59
Educational trips	60
Traveling: What an occasion!	60
Chart 5 Tooth brushing	61

ALIMENTARY ALLERGIES AND INTOLERANCES 62-70

What are they?	62
Chart 6 Some of the foods which are most likely to cause allergies and intolerances	64
Prevention	64
Diagnosis	67
What to do in case of proven allergy or intolerance?	68

PART II – RECIPES FROM THE WORLD, TO BE MADE FOR AND WITH YOUR CHILD

• Vegetable clear soup	72
• Rice cream	73
• Rice and fruit pudding	73
• Apple treat	74
• Pumpkin risotto	74
• Sesame flowers	76
• Green rice cake	77
• Ravioli	78
• Tomato sauce	80
• Pizza	80
• Oatmeal 'omelette'	82
• Crispy soy nuggets	83
• Baked felafels	84
• Potato gnocchi	85

- Avocado sauce — 86
- Mini veggy cakes — 86
- Peanut butter — 88
- Vegetarian paella — 88
- Hummus — 90
- Sesame sweets — 90
- Gram flour pizzas — 91
- Bottle gourd pizzas — 92
- Pumpkin fantasy — 93
- Mini sticks — 94
- Rainbow yoghurt — 94
- French pancakes (crèpes) — 95
- Almond cake — 96
- Biscuits — 97
- Yoghurt and fruit ice cream — 98
- Semolina cake — 99
- Chocolate almonds — 100
- Refreshing mint water — 100

BIBLIOGRAPHY — **102**

PART-I

A Bit of Know-how

The First Complementary Foods

Mothers–and fathers and grandparents–sitting in front of the paediatrist or chatting with other parents and caretakers in the local park, are often asked questions like: 'Has your baby started solids?' or 'Does your child eat?', 'What does he/she eat?' and 'How much?'

It seems like a delicate topic nowadays, where we all are quite concerned with the quantity of food consumed by our children and often busy in what could easily look like a race amongst mothers–whose child eats more and earlier? Which one is taller and–yes!– fatter?

This observation is not meant to make fun of one of the most natural instincts of parenthood.

Feeding the offspring is a perrogative of mothers of any species. It is associated with a deeply inbuilt instinct of care and preservation. It is also associated with love and emotions too, since it is the one act that creates and perpetuates the bonding between parents and kids, starting with the very first moments after birth, when a mother offers her breast to the tiny infant that by suckling tells her, 'I trust you, may your arms accompany me into this new world.'

Being concerned about our child's nutrition is absolutely positive and healthy but we should remember that children from all over the world (and this has been happening for millions of years) always learn to eat typical foods of their culture without much problem, and without their mothers and relatives getting stressed over the matter.

Our kids' meals should be approached with patience, common sense and extreme respect for their clues, preferences and needs. Often we confuse external schedules and dictates (like doctors' and grandparents' suggestions, or

our own expectations) with our kids' real needs.

At what age our babies should start eating solids and how much they should eat in a meal and during the day are decisions to be taken individually, by observing that particular child's real needs and demands.

Is your baby ready to start?

First of all, we should learn to recognize **when our baby is ready for the first complementary foods** that is, foods different from milk. These also include water and other beverages in case the baby is breastfed, since an *exclusively* breastfed infant does not need any other liquid other than mother's milk.

The World Health Organization recommends exclusive breastfeeding for *at least* six months. The same is applicable to bottle fed babies.

This is a 'minimum wait' criteria made on a medium range of children. It more or less helps to prevent allergies and other problems related to the early introduction of solids practised these days. This trend is a consequence of industrialization and availability of baby foods–like homogenized and dry frozen foods–that can be easily swallowed by infants who are indeed not yet ready for solids.

Note that such homogenized and dry frozen foods were initially meant for elderly people and other adults affected by health problems, like incapability to chew or swallow normal food. Only the growing power of industries and the economic interest lying behind it turned them into *baby foods*.

When a baby is really ready for solids, he will not need any of these special items. In many areas of the world, babies are still fed normal family foods, as their first solids– maybe just mashed with a fork, overcooked or cut small, or pre-chewed by the mother.

The First Complementary Foods

Given the general six months wait criteria, there are some more practical **signs to watch out for, in order to know whether our baby is ready for solids**—because we are human beings with individual differences, not machines built on a factory chain.

These signs are:

1. The baby can sit without support.
2. He is able to pick up food with his hands and put it in his mouth.

Riccardo

3. If a small quantity of food is placed on his tongue, he will move the tongue backwards and swallow it (the opposite movement is typical of suckling and it indicates that the baby is not yet ready to swallow solids. It does not mean that he dislikes that food).
4. The baby has some teeth or hard enough gums to chew and he makes a chewing movement with his jaws when something is in his mouth.

EASY FIRST FOOD

5. When offered, the baby is clearly able to refuse food (and such refusals shall be respected!).
6. The baby shows active and clear interest for our food (that is, he asks for it).

Complementation vs substitution

As adults, we are used to thinking of nutrition in terms of structured meals – breakfast, lunch, dinner, maybe a morning and/or afternoon snack.

When our baby will be approximately six months old, our paediatrist might suggest us to start substituting milk feeds with solids.

This *might* – and we underline **might** – work for bottle fed infants, who are mostly fed according to fixed time schedules and used to having *meals*.

Photographs by Ezio Conti. The baby horse alternatively eats grass and takes mother milk.

On the contrary, breastfed children nurse, rather than *having meals*. Their mother's breast is for them much more than nutrition: It is love, comfort, care and reassurance. Part of nursing is non-nutritive suckling, which is also very important for the child's development.

Breastfed children rarely have fixed nursing schedules (and this is how it should be!), because breast milk changes its composition according to the need of the moment, the child's hunger and thirst, his need to suckle for either nutrition or comfort... This makes the 'meal substitution' way of introducing solids counterproductive, first of all because these children are not used to meals.

Furthermore, substituting milk feeds with solids means weaning the child by hunger, which is unfair and unlikely to work in any case – no one would be eager to try something new, when starving. The child will most probably refuse the new food and desperately demand what he is used to (milk), engaging in a loop of anxiety.

The 'wean the baby by hunger' method is not recommended, not even in case the unfortunate baby accepts it. In fact, this method silences the natural capability of the child to self-regulate and recognize, by instinct, what is good for him.

Our babies know what they need much better than us, provided we do not keep offering them chocolates and other junks, just to see them eat as much as we desire!

Babies' refusals must be respected because they are not tantrums. Many a times, they indicate that the child is full or that his system is not yet ready for that particular food or it simply does not need it at that moment. Forcing the child might lead to severe problems like alimentary allergies or future incapability to self-regulate – and hence obesity, diabetes, etc.

We all know that hunger is a bad counsellor; it often makes us accept things that we would normally refuse to eat.

Solids should not be introduced by substitution, but by complementation. Let your child nurse or have milk according to his usual routine and slowly introduce solids as an addition to the normal quantity of milk.

At least initially, make sure to offer food to your baby

after he has had milk. This will preserve his self-regulation instinct and help prevent allergies and intolerances. It does not matter if he takes very little food (maybe just one or few spoons). It is fine. Kids need much less than we think.

If you are afraid of total alimentary anarchy, you may try to offer him solids every day around the same time, for example, when the rest of the family sits together for meals, or just before that. Nevertheless you should remember the 'complementation vs substitution' rule; a few sporadic exceptions will not harm, especially after the baby has already started accepting solids.

A Child Centered Meal

Once your baby has shown signs to be ready to start solids, you might be excited by the new steps being made and possibilities opening, by seeing your little bundle of joy growing towards independence. The same novelty might scare you as well, you might fear separation from the creature that till now has been so dependent on you, fear of breaking that special symbiotic bond that you two have been sharing during the first months of mother-child relation.

Such feelings are normal and there is no need to worry about them. Remember that if weaning happens gradually, with extreme respect for your child's and your own needs, it will not be a source of pain or anxiety. It will be just a step taken together to explore this new beautiful world.

During this period, you might be confused or overwhelmed by information received from different and sometimes disagreeing sources. What to give to your baby, what does he really need, how much, etc.

Vittoria

We will soon discuss these issues in a calm manner but let us first make some pedagogic premises. I am here talking about pedagogy because I believe that meals—and the way we approach them—play an educational role in the lives of our children. The first meals are not only the base of our

child's future health but also an occasion to learn by seeing, touching, smelling and doing. That is why we should be aware of their value and significance and find out the best way for our child to enjoy them.

The famous pedagogue Maria Montessori developed the insightful concept of making education child centered. This means that the child should be the main protagonist of educational practices, rather than a mere object bound to shape himself on other people's wills and musts. Sadly, education too often happens in this second way. We, as adults, have things to say, to teach, musts and no's that children have to conform to.

Children have great potential for self-learning and discovering the world. We should start observing them without prejudice to understand what they really need and the way they communicate. We might be surprised to see how much we can actually learn from them.

I believe that the meal is an educational moment, where intense family relations and emotions are involved. Much is learnt about our own cultural traditions and about nature and physics as well.

Since it involves educational processes, the meal should be child centered, too.

I neither like to be didactic nor prescribe ready-made life recipes. Just for the sake of exposing an idea effectively, briefly and understanding the meaning of this concept, I will now list a series of simple suggestions to make your child's meal child centered.

Learn to respect your child's appetite

Provided that you do not feed him junk, your child has a natural instinct which tells him when to eat, how much and what kind of food he needs at each particular moment of his life. Observe him carefully with understanding eyes, and follow his clues and needs.

Never force him to eat

This comes as an immediate consequence of the previous point. Once you have learnt to respect your child's appetite,

Lorenzo

you will not try to force him to eat when he is clearly trying to tell you to stop.

Imagine how you would feel, if someone tried to force you or even persuade you to eat or eat more, when your body is telling you: 'no' or 'enough'.

Avoid getting angry or scolding your baby, if he refuses to eat.

Avoid persuading the child by promising him a prize or a sweet. Having the child finish his meal by promising him a final sweet turns certain foods into prizes. This could have the side effect of teaching him to seek food as a compensation. It is very dangerous because it can cause

alimentary disorders – anorexia, bulimia, obesity…….during adulthood.

Avoid distracting your baby in order to make him eat passively (for example, force-feeding him while he is watching television or playing in the park).

Avoid following him for two hours all over the place to make him finish his meal, after he has clearly shown that his interest for the food is over.

Don't worry, he will not starve! If he is not interested in eating there is no point going on, beyond a point. Meals are intense educational moments, they should neither be consumed passively nor forcibly.

Of course there is no harm if a child, once in a while, eats in front of the television (all of us do it sometimes…) or if you want to read him a story or play a game while feeding him. Some children are easily distracted at such an early age. They might be slow eaters but lack the *patience* to sit and go on with their meal. We need to use a bit of common sense – if the child is bored by sitting there but he is otherwise still interested in the food, then let's be creative and make it fun!

Remember that if you respect your child now, you are giving him a life long precious gift – learning to follow his own appetite, and stop when satiated.

Just think about the growing number of obese and diabetic children all over the world. As you can see, there is more benefit in learning to stop when our tummy is full, rather than learning to keep ingurgitating even when we have had enough.

Do not rush

There is no hurry.

Start solids only when your baby is really ready and

A Child Centered Meal

Vittoria

then proceed slowly. If your child accepts the food and he does not show any sign of adverse reactions (for example, redness in the nappy area, vomit, diarrhoea, irritability...), increase the quantity.

Do not force your child to have too much food and too fast. Remember, like Louis Amstrong used to sing, that 'we have all the time in the world', 'time for life to unfold, time for love.'

We are not racing with other mothers but walking a path of discovery and love with our own child.

If you are still breastfeeding your baby on demand (and you are complementing his diet with solids, rather than trying to substitute breast milk with solids), you can be sure he is receiving all the nutrients he needs from your milk.

If your baby is formula fed by the age of six months he might need a bit more of solid complementation. But do not worry, as long as you feed him healthy, natural, iron rich stuff, his needs will be met, even if he takes very little in quantity.

If you are patient, you will see positive results in the future because your child will develop a healthy relationship with food.

Let him mess up a bit

Of course, we might like our child to learn good manners – and having less clothes in the daily laundry is not a bad

EASY FIRST FOOD

idea either. But there is time for all this. He will learn, but not now.

The first foods are a discovery and an adventure. Children explore with all five senses — taste, smell, touch, sight, hearing. They

Vittoria

need their hands to touch the food and feel its consistency. Eating with hands will also give our little explorer the feeling of importance coming from the achievement of doing it by himself, when his little hands might be still too clumsy for a fork or a spoon. Or he might want to imitate us by using that fork or spoon, but not succeed in reaching his mouth with the food.

It's fine. Let him try, let him learn.

Small children like to do things by themselves. If you stop them now, they might get so used to being fed that later it will be much more difficult to make them accept the idea of feeding themselves.

But most of all, if you never let them do, you deprive them of a first hand experience and relation with food.

I do not want to say that we should never feed our children. I do feed mine very often, with my own hands. Sometimes they do not want to eat food with a spoon but they accept it from my hands. It is a very sweet thing and it builds a bond between parents and kids. What I mean here is that we should not become so obsessed with hygiene and manners (or with speed/quantity of food consumed) that we never let our baby try and be on his own.

13

A Child Centered Meal

We grew up with the old ancient wisdom that one should not play with food. I think this saying is known more or less all over the world and I agree with it, to a certain extent. So many people are still dying of hunger; we must teach our children to respect food.

But let's not forget that for children, *playing* means *learning* and principles must be applied considering of the child's age, needs and understanding. If my four year old daughter starts throwing her rice all over the room I will most surely get irritated. But if my one year old son does the same I will probably try to save the food in a sweeter manner. Also, I will not really care if he eats with his hands or spreads the soup like a lotion on his face.

Given these premises, we all have to survive. And here are some useful **survival tips**, to prevent or reduce the frequency and intensity of disasters:

1. Do not put too much food in your baby's plate, neither too much water in his glass. In this way he will still be able to make his experiments but there is less to spread around. If he finishes and he wants more, you can always top it up later.

2. Spread old newspapers on the floor, under his chair and table. After the meal is over, you only have to throw the newspapers; you are saved of wiping the floor.

3. Use big, well covering bibs or a big T-shirt to wear on the normal clothes or a towel with an elastic band fixed on one side. My younger child refuses all these, so I simply resolved to keep a pair of old clothes aside, to be worn just for the meals.

Respect his preferences

Children's taste is very variable, so do not over worry on their refusals. Tomorrow they might hate today's favourite food and like something that they are rejecting now. Kids tend to be monothematic–only potatoes for a month and only carrots the next. It is normal and as long as you keep proposing a variety of healthy foods to the child, there is nothing to worry about. Every food can be substituted; none of them alone is indispensable. If your child does not like meat, he might accept pulses or eggs or fish; they are rich in proteins, too. If he does not want spinach, you might like to know that there is a lot of iron in so many other vegetables and fruits (for example, zucchini, broccoli, pumpkin, turnip, eggplant, apples, bananas…) and **even more** in egg yolks, meat, fish and pulses.

Do not insist too much if your child does not accept some particular food. This will only make him hate those foods, probably for the rest of his life.

This of course does not mean that you should go mad preparing ten different meals for him every time until he finds something suitable to his taste. A couple of options are more than enough. Just be a little flexible without pampering him excessively.

Of course, respecting your child's preferences refers to healthy foods; it does not mean that he should be allowed to survive on candies, burgers and chocolates.

Go healthy, no junks

Few transgressions here and there are always acceptable. In Italy, we have a proverb which says, 'the exception confirms the rule'– simply because it is identified as an *exception*.

Photograph by Ezio Conti

On the contrary, feeding our children junk to see them at least 'eating something' or 'introducing some calories' is diseducational and inexcusable. It teaches them wrong eating habits which might have a very dangerous impact on their future and present health. It intoxicates their little bodies without providing them the nutrients that they need to grow healthy.

Furthermore, it kills the child's natural capacity to self-regulate, which works only with natural healthy foods. Industrial processed foods make us feel satiated without giving us the nutrients that we need – or make us go on and on eating without realizing when it is time to stop. Sometimes they create an addiction, too. Many children are addicted to different kinds of industrial foods. This kills their interest for healthy stuff and may cause intoxication.

Just think of industrial sugars, for example, the old say that we should not have a candy before eating – this is not so wrong. Try and watch–your appetite will be reduced after eating the candy. The same happens with fried foods and similar stuff.

So, as much as you can:

1. Avoid junk foods (fried foods, industrial processed sweets and snacks, fast foods, canned sweetened juices, gassy and coloured drinks, candies….).
2. Avoid refined oils, margarines, trans fats and hydrogenated fats.
3. Avoid foods containing preservatives and artificial flavours (always read the label before buying a product).
4. Avoid excessive sugars.
5. Choose healthy crockery and healthy cooking methods, like steaming, grilling, baking, stewing, etc.
6. Do not overcook vegetables, leave them slightly crisp (except potatoes which are difficult to digest if under cooked), to prevent dispersion of nutrients.

Chart 1
Cooking methods

Boiling

It requires immersion of food in a large quantity of boiling water. It does not carry the negative side effects of frying, but it has the defect of dispersing vitamins and minerals contained in the food in the boiling water. Boiling is a good option for soups and clear soups, when the water in which the vegetables are being cooked will be consumed along with the food. It is good for cereals like rice, pastas, barley, etc. It can be chosen as an option in case of vegetables which require very quick boiling (one minute or less), before being used for other preparations (for example, broccoli). Green leaves can be immersed in boiling water and removed from it immediately (One second is just the time required for immersion).

Do not throw away the boiled water. It is full of vitamins and minerals. You can use it for other preparations like soups, cereals, pulses, etc.

Steaming

It is probably the healthiest cooking method. It presents all the advantages of boiling minus the defects. It ensures the maximum preservation of nutrients contained in the food. It is the optimum choice for vegetables, meat and fish. It can be done in specific steaming pans and utensils which keep the food far from the underlying boiling water or by cooking the food in a very small amount of water, just enough to be totally absorbed by the time the food is ready (in a pressure cooker or normal pan, with a cover).

Never throw away the steaming or boiling water. It is full of vitamins and minerals. You can use it for other preparations, like soups, cereals, pulses, etc.

Stewing

It is a slow method of cooking, which requires the minimum amount of oil, in a covered pan. It is a good option for certain kinds of meats, vegetables and pulses. You may or may not need to add water, according to the specific food.

Baking

It is a very healthy alternative to frying. Almost all traditional fried recipes (for example, omelettes, fish fingers, french fries...) can be made in an oven by keeping the temperature high and stirring frequently. Very little oil is required and the result is much healthier.

A good option for vegetables, meat and fish. Baked food is light, if you use little oil, and very tasty.

Indispensable for homemade cakes, biscuits, pizzas and breads.

Pressure cooking

It is a healthy and fast alternative to boiling and steaming. Optimum for pulses, which require very long cooking time with conventional methods. Good for vegetables (for example, potatoes), if very little water is used, and for rice preparations. Spinach and other green leaves are ready at the first whistle of the cooker and they do not require any water to be added.

Grilling

Quite a healthy choice for vegetables, meat and fish. It requires no oil or very little oil, according to your taste. Stir frequently and carefully; avoid carbonizing the food, because the burnt parts develop toxic substances.

Frying

It is not a healthy cooking method, since oils and any

other kind of fat tends to change their molecular composition when they reach high temperatures and this develops very toxic substances. Frying should be done with extreme moderation. Avoid frying in animal fats (butter, clarified butter, etc.) and choose unrefined vegetable oils with high smoking point, like extra virgin olive oil, mustard oil and coconut oil. Never burn the oil. If you see that the oil in which you are frying starts emitting a smelly smoke, throw it and start again with new oil. Never re-use the oil used for frying. Always throw it after having used it once.

Stir frying

It is a much healthier alternative to frying. It is done by cooking the food in a small amount of oil, for a very short time, stirring continuously. The optimum vessel for it is a wok. It is good for some kinds of vegetables in Asiatic preparations. Remember that the vegetables come out not totally cooked but slightly crisp – which helps them preserve their nutrients.

Relax and take care of the environment

Anxiety is a bad companion during meals. It kills the appetite and it causes bad digestion. Relax. Let it be a pleasant moment for your child and for yourself. Give him healthy stuff and do not over worry on the quantity of food he actually accepts. Do not force, do not get angry.

Exceptions are fine, but do not make watching television during meals a habit.

You do not need special crockery for your child's meal. Simple food grade plastics, steel or wood are unbreakable and perfectly okay.

A Child Centered Meal

Try to understand what arrangements are more suitable for the needs of your child and your own family. You might like to have the child eating at the table with you from the very beginning (with a high chair or a similar arrangement or even from your lap). In this way, he will observe you and learn to feed himself. Give him a small quantity of food at one time and let him do, while you eat your own food. Some children want to do it by themselves. Some others are very hungry and impatient, they want to be fed. Even this is fine.

You might, on the contrary find that the most suitable option for you is feeding your child alone, before the family eats, so that when you eat he is satiated and you can consume your meal in peace. There are no rules and even this solution can be good. Place the child where he is more comfortable (possibly not every time in front of the television), in a high chair, on the floor. You may setup a little table at his level.

Take care of the details, let the environment be pleasant and well settled. No one likes to eat on the go or in a messy atmosphere.

Do not leave him alone

This is a moment to enjoy each other's company, to socialize. Children do not like to eat in solitude. Be with them (you or another caretaker that you trust), so that they learn that food– and feeding – is love and care.

Photograph from the archive of 'In Grembo', Vercelli, Italy.

Not only food, they need to grow healthy

Open air, sun and nature are as important as food for your child's health and growth. (Note that sun is also important to synthesize vitamin D, which is indispensable for calcium absorption). Even if you live in a city, find

as many occasions as you can to take your child to nature, to big parks (and not only the polluted neighbourhood park!) or even out of the town itself. Search for nature and escape pollution. It might be a bit of a commitment on your side

Photograph by Ezio Conti.

but very much worth the effort because it will result in a positive health gain for your child and for the whole family.

Chart 2
A Note On Baby Foods

What we call baby foods, like homogenized or dry frozen foods, were initially meant for patients (mostly elderly patients) who were unable to chew or swallow normal food.

Boom of industrialization with related market interests extended the use of such preparations to a range of consumers who do not actually need them – infants. The result is a more and more precocious introduction of solids in the diet of babies who are not yet ready for the substances that are given to them.

When a child is ready for solids, he does not need this kind of stuff (refer – *Is your baby ready to start?*). If the whole family follows a healthy diet, normal family food will be perfectly fine for your baby. Initially, you may just keep out a potion for the baby, before adding too many condiments. Chopping the food with a knife or mashing it with a fork is enough. If your baby is ready, you do not need to grind it or homogenize it (this might also have the effect of habituing your child to foods with no chunks and later it might be difficult to wean him from this habit).

Furthermore, the quality of packaged baby foods is inferior to that of fresh homemade foods and their cost is much more expensive.

Here We Go!

In order to grow healthy, your child will need a balanced natural diet. This requirement is normally met by traditional local habits. Foods might vary according to geographic areas, but if a family consumes a variety of unprocessed healthy local foods, according to the culture of the place, the child's needs are normally met with.

Riccardo

Note that initially your child will just experiment. Do not expect him to consume big quantities of food and do not think of giving him complete meals immediately. Let him try different foods, explore real tastes. If you are complementing the usual milk diet with the new foods, you do not need to give him complex mixtures aimed at covering with that one meal, all his nutritional needs. Paediatricians used to prescribe mothers very funny recipes containing ingredients like, cereals, meat or pulses, vegetables and maybe oil and cheese– all mashed in one distasteful sort of pudding – that none of us would dare to eat! We are here starting a discovery adventure with our child, with the intent of sweetly introducing him to the colours, smells, tastes of mother nature and of our culture. Let's make it pleasant for him and uncomplicated for ourselves. Remember that if you complement instead of substitute, and if you start solids only and only when your baby is ready for them, then there is no need to worry about things taking long– your baby's nutritional needs are perfectly met with, if you continue breastfeeding him on demand.

Overview on nutrients

Carbohydrates

They give energy to your child's body and they are indispensable for all body functions.

They can be distinguished as digestible (amides and sugars) and non-digestible (fibres) carbohydrates. The first ones are processed in our liver and transformed in sugars, in order to give energy to our body. The second ones play a very important role in the functioning of intestines. **Vegetal fibres** ease intestinal transit and helps in preventing a lot of pathologies. They should always be present in a healthy diet, in a decent amount. Avoid an excess of vegetal fibres in a child's diet (especially in children below one year of age). They are found in all fruits and vegetables, whole cereals, pulses, nuts and oily seeds.

One should not abuse simple sugars (sweets, sugar, honey) because of the risk of pathologies like obesity, diabetes and dental cavities.

On the contrary, amides and complex carbohydrates should be the base for a healthy diet. They are essential for the functioning of a child's growing body.

They can be found in all cereals and derived products, pulses, nuts and tubers (for example, potatoes).

Proteins

They are made of chains of amino acids. Proteins are the main components of our body cells. They are indispensable for growth and renewal of tissues.

Essential amino acids cannot be synthesized by our body. They need to be introduced through food. Animal proteins contain all essential amino acids. Vegetal proteins, in order to be complete, need to be combined in one meal (whole cereals + pulses).

They are especially found in eggs, dairies, meat, fish, pulses, cereals, nuts and oily seeds.

Vitamins and minerals

They are essential for all body functions. Most of them cannot be synthesized by our body and they need to be introduced through food.

Deficiencies are responsible for several diseases. Vitamins and minerals must be introduced through a variety of healthy foods, which include plenty of fruits and vegetables (to be consumed cooked and raw too), cereals, pulses and/or meat/fish/eggs, dairies, vegetable unrefined fats derived by mechanical extraction, nuts, oily seeds and a small amount of animal fat.

Excesses can be dangerous too. For this reason we suggest to avoid integrators (these include tablets, syrups and several easily available drinks containing a mixture of proteins, vitamins and minerals), which are not meant to be substitutes of a varied diet but an aid in case of medical need, to be used under medical prescription and supervision.

Vitamin D (which plays an essential role in the metabolism of calcium and phosphorus and for this reason is indispensable for our children's bones and teeth) can be synthesized on exposure to the sun. For this reason, it is

very important that our children be regularly exposed to sunlight.

Vitamins are classified in two groups – lipo-soluble vitamins (A, D, E, K) that melt in fat. They are not eliminated through urine and their excess can cause dangerous health problems. The other group is hydro-soluble vitamins (B group, C, PP, M or folic acid) which melt in water. They are eliminated through urine and are stored in our body, only in a minimum quantity.

Certain minerals are toxic for our bodies. Minerals which are not toxic but indispensable for our health are calcium, iron, iodine, copper, cobalt, manganese, magnesium, sodium, potassium and selenium.

Fats

They cumulate in body's fatty tissues and are like an escort, ready to be transformed into energy when needed. They also serve as a vehicle for liposoluble vitamins. If excessive carbohydrates are introduced in our body, they are transformed into fat. Excess of fats can cause severe problems like obesity, heart and coronary problems and high cholesterol.

High cholesterol and circulatory diseases can be reduced or prevented by increasing the consumption of poly-unsaturated fats (found in vegetable oils) and by reducing the consumption of saturated fats (found in meat and animal fats, like butter, clarified butter, cream and fat cheese).

Chart 3
The Food Pyramid

The food pyramid is a general guideline to indicate the proportion in which foods from different categories should be consumed in a healthy diet. The foods at the base of the graphic should be the base of our diet while those at the top should be consumed with extreme moderation. Different versions have been made of such graphic, with slight variations. We report here the pyramid proposed in 1992 by USA (valid for omnivorous diets).

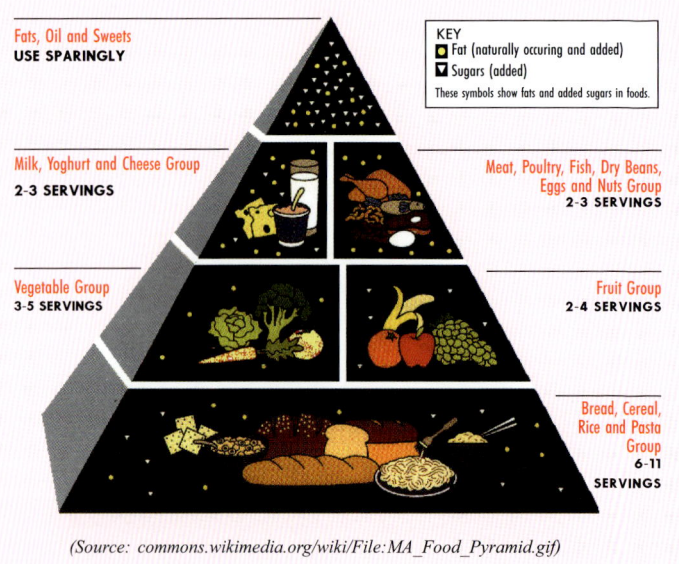

(Source: commons.wikimedia.org/wiki/File:MA_Food_Pyramid.gif)

Foods know-how

Keeping in mind that every child is unique and there cannot be any standard rule on how to proceed with foods, here are some general indications on first complementary foods. We suggest that you just read this as an example which has to be personalized and changed according to your child's and your family's needs and preferences.

As you will notice, the time schedules given below are very general, since we believe no calendar can meet the real needs of an individual child. Only mothers and other caretakers can know, by observing his clues, when a child is ready to make a new step or a new discovery.

The very first bites

WHAT?	HOW?	MORE...
Fruits Apple, pear, ripe, banana, apricot, melon	Mashed with a fork or grated or juiced. They can be served raw. Apples and pears can be cooked in a small quantity of water. This is a useful remedy in case of constipation. The water in which the fruit has been cooked can be drunk too.	They are a good source of vitamins and minerals.
Vegetables Pumpkin, carrots, zucchini or courgettes, bottle gourd, squash melon, fennel	Steamed or baked and mashed or in the form of clear soup (cooking water). Slowly more and more of the mashed vegetable can be added to the clear soup.	They are a good source of vitamins and minerals. Their sweet taste (especially that of carrots and pumpkin) is normally liked by children.

Here We Go!

Beginnings

WHAT?	HOW?	MORE…
Fruits Papaya, plums, grapes, watermelon	Mashed or grated, cut in small pieces, cut in slices when the fruit is ripe and soft. In this case, remember to remove the skin and seeds to avoid suffocation. Fresh juices (without added sugars) can be given too	They are a good source of vitamins and minerals. Papaya and plums might have a laxative effect.
Vegetables Potato, sweet potato, lettuce, spinach and green leaves, cabbage, cauliflower, broccoli, turnip, beetroot	Steamed or baked and mashed or in the form of clear soup. Slowly more and more of the mashed vegetable can be added to the clear soup. You can also serve them to the child after cutting them into small pieces or in soft slices to bite (this works very well with steamed or baked pumpkin slices). You can start giving the child grated raw vegetables as well (for example, carrot, fennel).	They are a good source of vitamins and minerals. Note that breastfed children normally accept very easily vegetables whose taste is strong (for example, cabbage, turnip, cauli-flower), if they got used to it from their mother's milk.

EASY FIRST FOOD

WHAT?	HOW?	MORE…
Cereals Rice, corn	Whole cereals over cooked and, in the case of corn, dehulled. They can be mashed or ground to prepare creams which can be mixed with fruits or vegetables. The cereals can also be cooked directly in vegetable clear soup. Flours and flakes to be cooked in vegetable clear soup, apple juice or water.	They are a source of carbohydrates and minerals. Corn is very rich in iron. Using whole brown rice provides a better intake of minerals and fibres.

WHAT?	HOW?	MORE…
Pulses Dehulled lentils	Cooked in plenty of water or clear soup.	They are a good source of proteins, iron and other minerals. Combined with whole cereals (for example, lentil soup with brown rice cream), they provide a complete range of amino acids (proteins).

WHAT?	HOW?	MORE…
Meat Prefer non-fat, white meat (like chicken and rabbit)	Steamed and ground or mashed or cut into small pieces (according to the child's age and capability to chew; older children can be given a chicken leg to chew). Meats can also be served in the form of soups and clear soups.	It is a good source of proteins and iron. Nevertheless, meat is not essential and it can be substituted by pulses combined with whole cereals (later with dairies, eggs and fish).

Here We Go!

Later

WHAT?	HOW?	MORE...
Fruits Mangoes, strawberries, berries, figs, kiwis, oranges and other citrus fruits, cherries, pomegranate, dry.	Cut in pieces or slice (remove seeds); juiced. Dry fruits can be given the way they are to be chewed, cut in small pieces or softened in water (the water where they have been soaked can be drunk too). They can also be used as sweeteners in other preparations (puddings, biscuits and cakes, yoghurt).	They are a good source of vitamins and minerals. Pomegranate is an excellent source of iron. If the child has not yet developed a good chewing ability, avoid giving him the small seeds; prefer juicing the fruit, to prevent risk of suffocation. Citrus fruits, berries, strawberries and cherries are very rich in vitamin C, but they might cause allergies. Introduce them late (when the child is about one year old), especially if someone in the family is allergic to them. Dry fruits are very energizing and a good source of vitamins and minerals. Since they contain a lot of sugar, care should be taken in cleaning teeth after consuming them.

EASY FIRST FOOD

WHAT?	HOW?	MORE...
Vegetables Tomatoes, eggplant, bitter gourd, fenu-greek, peppers, radish and wild radish, asparagus, mushrooms, onions, garlic, leak, okra, french beans.	Steamed or baked; raw and grated or cut very thin.	They are a good source of vitamins and minerals. Tomatoes might cause allergy. Introduce them late (when the child is about one year old), especially if someone in the family is allergic to them.
Cereals Wheat, oat, barley, amaranth millet, sorghum, rye.	Flours are to be cooked in water or as clear soups; can also be used in other preparations. Flakes, semolina, pasta, couscous, bulghour can be cooked in water or clear soup.	They are an excellent source of carbohydrates, proteins (if combined with pulses) and minerals. These group of cereals contain gluten, a factor which might cause allergies. For this reason, it is very important not to introduce them too early in the child's diet. The child should be minimum 6-7 months old, but in case any relative suffers from coeliac disease (intolerance to gluten), the waiting period should be extended to atleast one year of age. The post-ponement of introduction of cereals

31

| | | containing gluten should be accompanied by prolonged breastfeeding, which is the best way to prevent any kind of allergy and intolerance. |

WHAT?	HOW?	MORE...
Pulses Beans, grams, soy and derived products, lentils, peas.	To be initially dehulled to avoid gassy colic, they can slowly be given with their skin as the child grows.	Excellent source of proteins and minerals.
Fish	Steamed or baked.	It is an excellent source of proteins, minerals and omega 3 fatty acids, which protect against high cholesterol, heart and circulatory diseases. Tips to recognize fresh fish: • The eye is brilliant, not opaque. • The skin is compact and it does not come off if touched. • The gills have a good red color inside. • It smells of fish, but it does not smell bad or rotten or raw; neither while cooking.

EASY FIRST FOOD

WHAT?	HOW?	MORE...
Nuts and oily seeds Almond, walnut, hazelnut, coconut, pine-nut, peanut, cashew, chestnut.	To be initially given in the form of spreadable creams or flours to be used in several preparations, to avoid suffocation.	They are very energetic, an excellent source of carbohydrates, proteins, vitamins and minerals; they are a good source of fats also. Six almonds have the nutritional value of a steak! They are a perfect dietary integration in case of stress and tiredness.
Eggs	Boiled or half boiled or 'fried' without oil in a non-stick pan. Oil-free omelettes can be made in a non-stick pan or in the oven, plain or with vegetables, boiled rice or pastas inside. A tip to prevent allergies – the first time you feed your child an egg start with a bit of yolk (less than half a teaspoon); if you do not observe any reaction, gradually increase the dose day by day.	They are a very nutritious food, very rich in proteins (in the white), minerals (especially iron, which is contained in the yolk), fats (again in the yolk), and some vitamins (but not vitamin C). Individuals who suffer from cholesterol or are overweight should consume them in moderation or avoid the yolk. Normal growing children can eat upto 4-5 eggs a week. Eggs can cause allergies.

Here We Go!

	Introduce the white after being sure that your child tolerates the yolk well, (although it is easier to digest, the most allergy causing part of the egg are the proteins contained in the white).	Introduce them after nine months and, in case someone in the family is allergic, after one year.

WHAT?	HOW?	MORE...
Dairies Milk, yoghurt, cheese.	Cow's milk is not indispensable, but if the child likes it, it can be given in the glass, tepid or cold. It can be used to make porridges and other preparations. Yoghurt can be given natural, with fruits or honey. Avoid readymade, flavoured yoghurts. Prefer fresh, non-fermented cheese, low in fat (for example, cottage cheese). Avoid all those spreadable varieties of cheese which are derived from the fusion of other dairy products and those containing colourants and preservatives.	Dairies are a very common cause of allergy; cow milk proteins are different from human milk proteins. Their chain of amino acids is longer and they are more difficult to digest. It is better to introduce cow's milk after the child is one year old. This problem is less severe in the case of yoghurt, because it is pre-digested. Some people may also be intolerant to lactose, the sugar contained in milk.

Condiments

Vegetal fats

Choose traditional cold pressed oils (that is, derived from mechanical extraction), like extra virgin olive oil, sesame oil, mustard oil, peanut oil, groundnut oil, etc. They are a good source of fats, vitamins and minerals.

Avoid margarines, refined oils, hydrogenated oils and trans fats, because their chemical composition is altered and extremely dangerous for health.

Animal fats

Butter and clarified butter should be consumed in moderation. They are a good source of vitamin A but they also contain high levels of cholesterol. They should always be consumed uncooked; adding them when the meal is ready. They should not be cooked and they must never be used for frying, because their chemical composition changes very quickly with heat, turning them into real health hazards.

Sweeteners

Refined sugar should be avoided (it increases the risk of diabetes, obesity and tooth decay).

Honey, unrefined brown sugar or dry fruits are better substitutes to sweeten our kids' and our own dishes.

Salt

It should be introduced as late as possible in a child's diet. It should be used with extreme moderation. Don't overload their small kidneys. This precaution will also teach them to appreciate the foods' natural taste.

Spices and herbs

Local varieties of spices and herbs are used all over the world for cooking. They all have different beneficial properties and they are a good alternative to salt and other condiments.

Beverages

The best beverage for a thirsty child is plain still water. Water is essential for life, and it provides a series of important minerals, although unfortunately many of them are eliminated through the purifying processes, which are often indispensable to turn contaminated water into drinking water. If this is the case in your geographic area, you should take care of introducing higher quantities of minerals through food (by consuming plenty of fresh fruits, vegetables, whole cereals, pulses, etc.).

Avoid sweetened juices and canned soft drinks. Go for fresh juices, lime water, herbal teas, barley 'coffee' (made out of toasted barley flour).

Veg or non-veg?

Meat and fish are a good source of proteins and iron. Nevertheless, they are not indispensable for the child. In many areas of the world, people have been growing healthy vegetarian children, because of cultural traditions and religious beliefs.

If your child is vegetarian but includes animal products like dairies and eggs (if you have doubts on how to classify eggs, remember that *unfertilized eggs*–that is, coming from a farm where a cock is not present–do not contain any *baby*! In this case the content of the eggs is simply the *food* that was destined to be the baby but the baby was actually never conceived), your child will definitely grow healthy, without any risk of alimentary deficiencies.

In case the baby is on a strict vegetarian diet – vegan diet, that is, a diet which excludes any product of animal origin – your child might miss some nutrients and he

might need integrations. Vitamin B12 is very important for the neurological development of children and to maintain good levels of haemoglobin in the blood. This vitamin is present in sufficient quantity only in animal products, may it be meat, fish or even just eggs and/or dairies. If you follow a vegan diet, your child's health should be carefully monitored by a specialist (a paediatrist), to be sure that he is not at risk.

Remember that even omnivorous children and adults (that is, people eating non-vegetarian food too) should not exceed meat intake–twice a week is more than enough (prefer non-fat white meat like chicken or rabbit).

If your choice does not depend on religious beliefs, we suggest you to be flexible and respect your child's preferences. Like we have already said, no particular food is indispensable and everything can be substituted.

If you are vegetarian, but your child does not like pulses, you might try some meat or fish or eggs. Some children have a body constitution that does not allow them to eat too much all at once and they might need several small meals made of highly nutritious concentrated foods, like eggs or meat. Or you might be a meat eater and have a child who simply hates meat. Try something else. Respect your child, learn to observe him and understand his clues and, more than all, put his health before your personal convictions.

How much do children really need?

How much food a child really needs to eat can be suggested only by his own body constitution and appetite. Children are different from each other (like adults are, too) and they have different needs. Some of them might need and want a lot, some others very little. Their appetite varies. There will be days, months or years when they will eat more, then periods in which they will eat less.

Children require more calories during periods of fast growth (growth sprints). After they are one year old their growth rhythm slows down (this is normal and healthy) and many children start needing less. Picks of fast growth will occur again around the third year of age and during adolescence (but again, these are not fixed schedules and the pattern varies from child to child). Here, our child might magically start to eat a lot.

As these are just tendencies and not mathematical rules, do not worry if your child remains a fussy eater or a permanently hungry one. As long as you feed him healthy stuff, in a healthy relaxed atmosphere – and you take care of having him spend lots of time in nature, sun and open air – there is nothing to worry. Just avoid feeding him junk, to simply see him introducing some calories.

Are you sure that he is really not eating?

We frequently hear mothers complaining that their child does not eat enough. When I ask them to tell me what all does the same child eat in a day, I am often surprised to see that their child is in fact having a lot more than mine!

This is not to minimize a natural concern that we all have towards our children's nutrition. We are concerned because we love them and it is fine. The only problem is that the same preoccupation, when it becomes excessive, turns meal times into real sources of stress and anxiety, for us and – worse – for our children.

I am sure all of us want meals to be a happy enjoyable moment, a pleasant family memory and not an hour of struggle. For this to happen, we need to reduce our expectations. A small body needs much less than an adult. Remember, like the Spanish paediatrist Carlos Gonzales points out, that it *is not true that children eat to grow*. It is indeed the contrary: *they eat more when they are growing*, in order to sustain the fast speed of growth. It is a subtle difference, but it is illuminating and such a relieving discovery for us worried mothers.

Small stomachs have space just for small quantities of easily digestible and nutritious food. Overloading them can only cause refusals, bad digestions, vomiting and belly ache.

Growth

Children grow at different speeds and at different ages. As we said many times, they are individuals and not easily predictable machines.

As long as they are healthy, smart and playful there

Cecilia

is nothing to worry if they are not as tall or big as our neighbour's. They will grow later and how much they will grow is mostly related to their genetic potential. If the parent's constitution is not so big, you cannot expect the child to be a giant. Food does not make a big difference, except in case of real malnutrition (remember that a child who is fed a lot of junk is as malnourished as one who does not eat at all, although he might look fatter than the last).

We report here the percentile growth curves made by WHO (World Health Organization), which are at the moment the most updated and reliable ones. Sadly, many paediatrists still use old charts, creating unneeded confusion and panic in concerned parents. We suggest that you monitor your baby's growth according to these charts. Before panicking, be sure of what charts your paediatrist is using to assess your child's growth.

Remember that percentiles have been made on a huge population of healthy children. Even if your child is placed on a very low percentile, it means that there are hundreds of healthy children who are smaller than him. If the child

EASY FIRST FOOD

is growing slow but steadily there is nothing to worry.

If your child is out of the percentile range, it indicates that a health check up is required, but it does not necessarily mean that he is sick. Some children are just small, but they are perfectly healthy and smart.

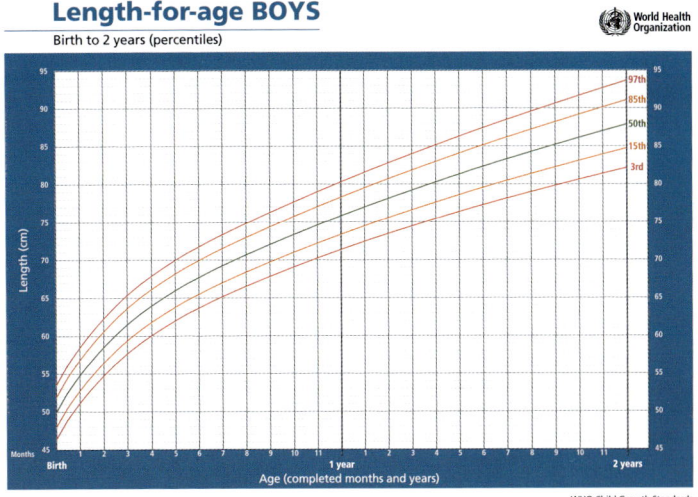

(Source: www.who.int/childgrowth/standards/en/)

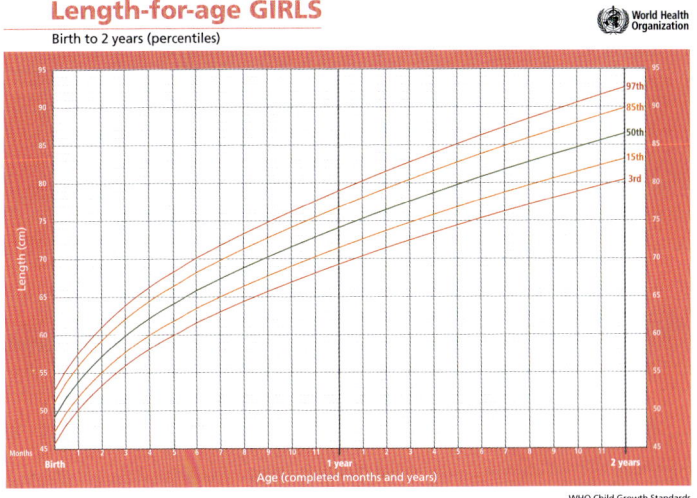

(Source: www.who.int/childgrowth/standards/en/)

Growth

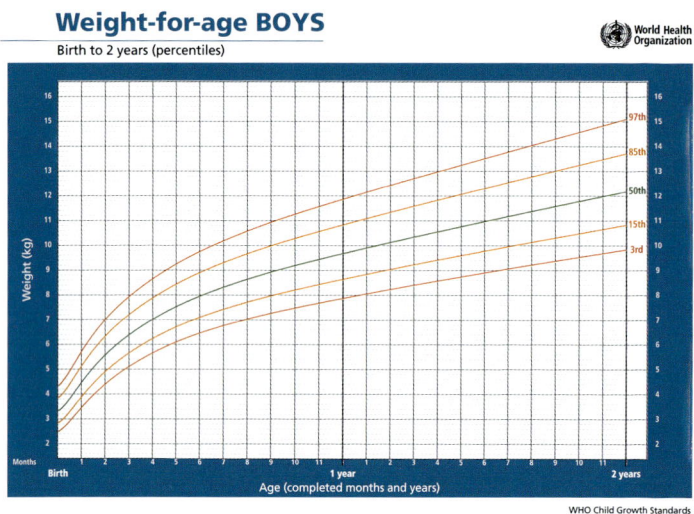

(Source: www.who.int/childgrowth/standards/en/)

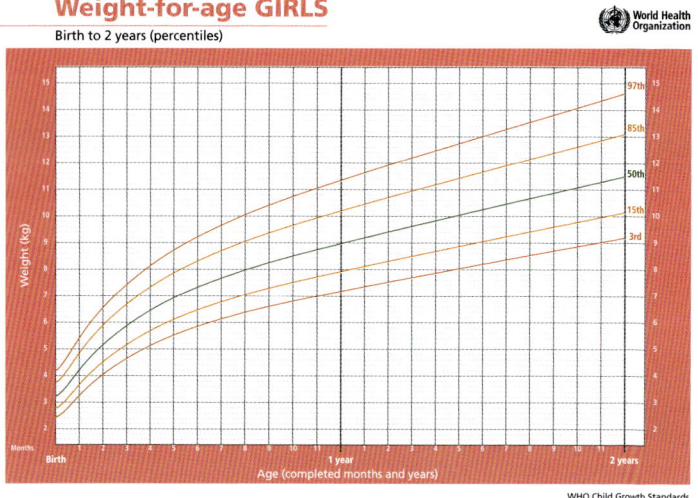

(Source: www.who.int/childgrowth/standards/en/)

Foods For Growth

As we mentioned above, healthy growth requires a healthy diet. Malnutrition does not merely indicate scarcity of food intake but also refers to bad diets – i.e. unbalanced and/or excessive and/or made up of junk foods.

It might seem like an obvious observation, but we shall remember that yes, kids might insist on having junks, but certainly they cannot buy them on their own. There is a high degree of parental responsibility regarding the kids' access to junk food. It is true that our children will in any case come in touch with such unhealthy stuff from friends, relatives and other people in the society. And we are personally convinced that few trangressions are allowed – if they are really few, they simply comfirm the rule. Nevertheless it is very important to give to the new generations a good example within the family, to habitue kids to healthy choices and explain them "why". If they are treated with respect and trust, kids are perfectly capable of understanding.

Read labels, always. Explain your children the reasons to prefer certain foods over others. When they will be big enough to read, they will do this on their own. You will be amazed to see how a small child can be responsive to the message, if this is given with balance and convinction. Just a few days back, my five year old daughter spontaneously refused certain sweets that a friend had offered her because, she told me: "They contain those bad trans oils". My nephew surprised her mother, during a phone call from her college, when she told her: "I just bought apples, because I was feeling fatigued". Apples, as my sister in law had taught her daughter for years without apparent immediate result, not chocolates!

Given this premise, all healthy foods are useful because of their different properties. We should habitue our kids to a wide variety of healthy foods, without forcing them if they reject something. Slowly, if they are exposed to different natural foods, they will learn to try new flavors and appreciate them. When they will be grown up, they will remember and understand.

Fruits

Amla

It has great medicinal value because it is extremely rich in ready to assimilate vitamin C. It is cooling, diuretic and regulative of intestine. It also contains some proteins, vitamin A, calcium, iron. It can be consumed in the form of jams, chutneys, candies, pickles or even chopped and added raw on foods, soups, salads.

Guava

It is very rich in vitamin C. Laxative, especially if eaten whole, without peeling or eliminating seeds.

Citrus Fruits (oranges, lemons, etc.)

Poor of sugars (less than 10%), they give a high intake of vitamin C (30/50 mg/100gr).

If consumed in winters at least once a day they prevent infections. They act against vessels diseases and capillaries fragility. Their high potassium content is responsible for their diuretic effect.

Oranges are especially helpful against tiredness, throat and ear infections and flu. Citric acid improves digestion and iron absorption.

Mango

Very nutritious, it should be consumed in moderation in case of diabetes and obesity because it is very rich in sugars. It contains a good amount of vitamin A, C, G and iron. It is laxative and diuretic.

Papaya

It improves digestion and contains a good amount of

vitamin A, B, C, D. It contains minerals, especially calcium, iron, phosphorus. Helpful in case of constipation, digestive problems and kidney stones.

Pomegranate

Very rich in iron, sugar, citric acid. It seems to be helpful in case of diarrhoea.

Apricot

Mildly rich in sugars (10%), it is low in calories when consumed fresh, but five times more when consumed dry.

It is interesting for:

- sporty people (rich in potassium, it prevents cramps)
- students (rich in phosphorus)
- prevention of cancer and cells aging
- it improves crepuscular vision

Pineapple

Very rich in fibres, it is good for digestion and drainage. It has an anti-inflammatory action. Keep attention to allergies.

Watermelon

In spite of its sweet taste it is not very rich in sugars. It is not very caloric. If consumed in a balanced diet it has a diuretic and depurative effect. Rich in fibres it gives a feeling of satiety. Thanks to the high content of water it prevents summer dehydration.

Kiwi

Its content in vitamin C is double the quantity contained in an orange. Only one kiwi can cover the daily need of an individual. It is rich in fibres and has laxative properties. It contains a lot of minerals but it is very allergenic.

Banana

It is rich in sugars, calories and potassium. Dried banana is richer in minerals than the fresh one. It is very nutritious and is often consumed by sporty people because it is rich in potassium and magnesium. It also helps in muscular contraction.

Grapes

Rich in vitamins and minerals. Diuretic and purifying, it improves blood vessels resistance. It is very energetic so diabetics should keep attention.

Apple

It stimulates kidneys and intestine and facilitates digestion. It has a well known anti cholesterol action. It is helpful in preventing tooth decay. It contains a low amount of vitamin C.

Melon

It is rich in beta carotene (precursor of vitamin A) and contains high quantity of vitamin C and potassium. It is diuretic and laxative, rich in water and low in calories.

Lemon

Very rich in vitamin C, it prevents winter infections, cold, sinus, flu. Its regular consumption improves vessels tone. It also prevents bones decalcification.

Dry Fruits

Very high in calories, to be consumed with moderation in case of diabetes and overweight. Their lipids are important for the prevention of cardiovascular diseases. They lower cholesterol and have a good antioxidant effect.

Vegetables

Aubergine

It is recommended in case of weak intestine and diabetes. It is low in calorie thanks to its high water content. It prevents cardiovascular diseases.

Spinach

They are not so rich in iron like it is commonly believed, but they contain vitamin B9 which improves iron absorptions. They are rich in vitamins and minerals (potassium, magnesium, calcium).

Pumpkin And Zucchini

Low in calories, diuretic, mildly laxative. They are very rich in water and contain a good amount of vitamins and minerals.

Beetroot

Rich in glucides, potassium, folic acid. It has a diuretic effect. Prevents and treats anaemia.

Broccoli

They are rich in fibres and facilitate intestinal transit. They are rich in vitamin A and C with antioxidant properties. It seems to prevent cancer and cardiovascular diseases. It is advised in case of anaemia.

Carrot

It is low in calories and rich in carotene which gives it its typical orange colour. It is available all round the year. It contains a good amount of natural sugars, for this reason it should be consumed with moderation in case of diabetes. It is rich in vitamins, fibres and minerals. It is useful in case of intestinal infections and diarrhoea.

Cabbage

It is the king of vegetables, in all its varieties (green, white, red, cauliflower, broccoli, etc). It is a winter vegetable rich in vitamin C (an orange has at least thrice less vitamin C than 200 grams of cabbage). It is low in calories and useful in case of constipation. It is recommended in case of anaemia. It has anti carcinogenic properties (intestine and stomach). It should be consumed with moderation in case of goitre or thyroid dysfunction.

Cucumber

Low in calories, rich in water. Detoxicant and astringent for the skin. It contains mineral salts like potassium, calcium, phosphorus.

Capsicum

Low in calories, rich in water, minerals and vitamin C, B9, beta carotene. Red capsicum contains three times the amount of vitamin C than an orange, while the green one only double.

Tomato

Mildly laxative and low in calories. Poor of glucides, it contains many minerals and oligo elements.

Turnip

Rich in fibres, diuretic, it helps to prevent kidney stones. It prevents cancer and is a good source of vitamin C. It contains sugars, proteins, antioxidant and detoxifying substances.

Cereals

Chose whole cereals: being unrefined their nutritional value remains unaltered. Unrefined cereals are especially rich in magnesium (useful in case of cramps and tiredness),

mineral salts and B group vitamins.

Wheat

It is a nutritional treasure. It is the most cultivated cereal and is the base of many foods. It has complete glucides, vegetal proteins, B group vitamins, minerals and fibres.

Rice

Very easy to digest cereal, it contains a low amount of proteins. Especially the white polished one is nutritionally inferior to the whole brown grain, since most vitamins and minerals are contained in the external layer. White rice can be useful in case of diarrhoea.

Oat

It is a very caloric cereal, often consumed in the shape of flakes, especially for breakfast.

Rich in proteins (higher quantity than other cereals), minerals, vitamins and fats. Advised for children and sporty people, if not allergic. It cannot be consumed in gluten free diets.

Ragi

Very easy to digest, it contains a good amount of carbohydrates and proteins and is very rich in calcium. Particularly indicated in case of diabetes, because it contains iodine which slows the absorption of glucose.

Jowar

Very rich in B vitamins complex but poor in calcium, it contains carbohydrates and proteins like other cereals.

Corn

Less rich in proteins than wheat but rich in iron, it contains a certain amount of vitamin A. Slightly laxative. It can be consumed steamed, roasted or in the form

of popcorn, a healthy snack for all ages if prepared without oil or butter or with a small quantity of oil from mechanical extraction. Mind the industrial ready to pop (in microwave or pressure cooker) varieties available in the market because they contain dangerous hydrogenated oils.

Millet

Easy to digest cereal, low in fats and very rich in proteins. It contains sugars, fibres, vitamins, a lot of potassium useful for cerebral cells activity.

Barley

It regulates intestine. It is poor in fats, rich in proteins and fibres. It is very useful in case of infant constipation.

Boulghour

It is a whole wheat, pre sprouted, pre cooked and dried, typical of macrobiotic diets. It is rich in amid, vegetal proteins, vitamin E and B, minerals, iron, magnesium, potassium, phosphorus.

Pulses

Rich in vegetal proteins and fibres, they facilitate intestinal transit. Their low glycemic index induces weak insulin stimulation. They can be consumed in case of diabetes and overweight.

Lentils

Very important for their high protein content. They can substitute meat and they balance vegetarian diets. They are rich in potassium and other mineral salts.

Grams

Very rich in vegetal proteins, they are a core food in vegetarian diets. They contain sugars and a high amount of fats.

Beans

They are a good source of vegetal proteins, poor in fats but rich in fibres, B group vitamins and minerals. When combined with cereals they become a high nutritional meal.

Soya

It is very rich in proteins (double than lentils) and with these it can cover the whole body need. Combined with a cereal it can substitute meat. It can prevent cancer (especially at colon level). It lowers the risk of cardiovascular problems.

Tofu

Cheese derived from soymilk, it is rich in proteins and advised in vegetarian diets. Rich in calcium and magnesium, it does not contain cholesterol.

Sprouts

They can be obtained by all pulses, cereals and seeds. They are the vital force concentrated in germination. All the properties of the seed are increased, because the content of vitamins and mineral salts is considerably higher. That is why they should be included in all diets.

Eggs

It would be an almost complete food if it did not lack sugars and vitamin C. The white is an excellent source of proteins, very easy to digest if not excessively cooked. The yolk is important for the formation of cell membranes and nervous system. It is a good source of vitamin A, B12 and B9. It is rich in iron, folic acid, fats.

Dairy Products

Milk

It is the first choice for healthy food if it comes from

organic farming. Otherwise it can be highly contaminated by cattle drugs. It is mostly formed of water and contains sugars, fats, proteins, mineral salts, vitamin A and D.

Cheese

Derived from milk, it is very rich in calcium. It is also very rich in sodium and saturated fats. That is why it is better to consume it with moderation. Goat or sheep cheese can be a good substitute in case of intolerance to cow milk. One should give attention to avoid all industrial varieties available in the market which are normally adulterated with colorants and preservatives and often obtained by industrial dairies residuals.

Buttermilk

More digestible than milk, it contains almost all its nutrients except fats. Helpful in case of diarrhoea and digestive problems.

Fish

It contains proteins of high biologic value. It prevents cardiovascular diseases. Studies on Eskimos demonstrated that by consuming a lot of fish, mortality by heart attack is reduced to the minimum. It has been demonstrated that consuming fish thrice a week reduces half the risk of coronary disturbances.

NUTS

Almonds

They are very energetic. They contain mono unsaturated fats whose action benefits cardio vascular system. They are very rich in lipids, minerals, magnesium, potassium, iron, calcium.

Walnuts

They contain poli unsaturated fatty acids, phosphorus, magnesium, vitamin E and B, that is why they should be introduced in our diet, adding them to salads or in the form of oil.

Coconut

Very nutritious, particularly rich in vitamin A, B1 and G, potassium, sodium, magnesium, iron, phosphorus, sulphur. Rich in fat, it contains a moderate quantity of carbohydrates and proteins. Its water is diuretic and purifying, helpful in case of stomach ache and gastritis. Coconut milk can be used in cooking, to substitute oil and butter.

Sesame

It is the food of brain and memory. Its seeds contain fats, calcium, zinc and selenium, proteins and fibres. It can be used on salads or in the form of oil.

Condiments

Vegetal Oils

Cold pressed varieties are rich in mono unsaturated and polyunsaturated fatty acids, which are helpful in reducing cholesterol.

Oils Of Animal Origin

Fish oil helps in lowering the level of lipids in the blood and it has a beneficial effect on vessels. Other kinds of animal fats like lard should be avoided because they are too rich in saturated fats.

Butter and clarified butter

A good source of vitamin A. Butter contains some proteins as well. They should be consumed in moderation (especially in case of high cholesterol) and always raw.

Honey

It has a superior sweetening power than sugar. It contains fructose, a slow absorption sugar. It helps in case of throat and bronchial infections and it carries the beneficial properties of the plants from which it derives. It is a very nutritious food, to be used with moderation in case of diabetic familiarity.

Raw sugarcane

It is energetic and rich in iron. To be preferred over refined sugars.

Salt

Do not abuse it. Choose iodized salt (effective to prevent goitre and hyperthyroidism) or raw salt (very rich in oligo elements).

Herbs and Spices

Onion

Like garlic, it has anti aggregative properties on blood plasters. Raw onion lowers plasters aggregation and increases the duration of bleeding. It lowers cholesterol and has an antioxidant and vermifuge and antiseptic action.

Garlic

Important aromatic plan used for garnishing. It acts on plasters with anti aggregative properties (anti thrombosis effect which prevents artery occlusion and protects from heart diseases). It also inhibits the enzyme responsible for the synthesis of cholesterol. It favours vessels dilation in case of artery hypertension and has a light diuretic action. The antioxidant effect makes it useful to prevent aging and to fight chronic diseases like cancer. It also has vermifuge and antiseptic properties.

Mint

It improves digestion. Since it has a stimulating effect on the nervous system, it is better not to consume it in the evening.

Into Toddlerhood And Further

Learning and fun with food

If food is discovery and exploration, this is most valid during toddler years, when children seem so eager to know and to do, that we often find ourselves saying, "Will he ever stop for a minute?"

This is a time of intense learning, where good eating habits and a healthy enjoyable relationship with food can be more easily formed.

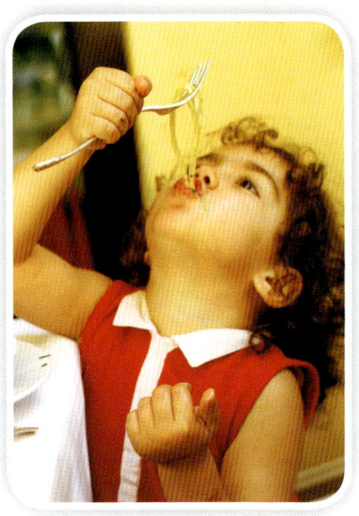

Caterina

Here are some fun ideas to help your toddler (and also your older child) learn and enjoy with food.

Going grocery shopping with your child

When you go for groceries, take your child with you. Let him see what is available, the foods, the colours. Let him choose (healthy stuff). He will like to eat what he has chosen by himself.

He will have a different kind of outing and he will learn to recognize foods and name them. He will learn to measure quantities as well.

When he starts writing and reading, you may ask him to help you prepare a shopping list before going out. This will make him feel responsible and it will also be a good reading/writing exercise.

EASY FIRST FOOD

Cooking with your child

This is an activity that kids normally enjoy a lot. They like imitating you and most of all they like manipulating different kinds of objects and materials, because this is their way of learning. Dress them with old clothes or cover them with a 'cooking uniform' and let them enjoy. Don't worry if they get dirty or mess up the kitchen (you can always ask them to help you clean afterward; this is again an activity that they normally do with pleasure).

There are many things that a toddler can do. You can ask him to beat the eggs for an omelette, to wash or cut (with supervision) soft or boiled vegetables. A small child can help you measure food quantities and he will be introduced to mathematics. Reading recipes will be a good exercise for preschoolers and older children.

Seeing foods change their characteristics while cooking will introduce physics transformations.

Doing is probably the best way of learning and your child will be happy and proud of eating (and see other family members eating) something that has been cooked with his contribution.

Decorating dishes

Ask your child to place food in dishes and decorate them with raw vegetables, cheese cubes, boiled pulses or other stuff. You might teach him how to colour boiled eggs using natural substances like beetroot juice (pink colour) or turmeric paste (yellow colour). Let your fantasy run free. Your child will use his creativity and build a connection with the food. Children are normally very creative and they enjoy these kind of crafts.

Inventing recipes

This is again a good way to develop your child's creativity. It also helps him discover local foods and build a personal relation with them. Guide him on food combinations and let him explore and invent new solutions according to his taste. You will be amazed to see the small chef inside him!

Older children can help by writing down and reading recipes, along with taking out the quantities of ingredients (in numbers or by using simple measuring units like cups, glasses, spoons). It can also be an occasion for counting, measuring and weighing ingredients.

Playing the restaurant game

Let your child set the table nicely for the whole family and ask him to help you serve the food with style. While in the previous game he was the chef, now he plays the waiter role. This will help him feel responsible towards others and develop an active relationship with food.

Going for picnics

Going for picnics is enjoyable for both adults and children. It has the benefit of being in the open air, close to nature and it is a change of setting which eliminates the

EASY FIRST FOOD

monotony factor that children often associate with meals. It is an occasion for family members and friends to spend time together. Sharing meals always help people in creating bonds or making them stronger.

A nice idea for picnics (and parties as well) is asking all the invitees to prepare something, maybe according to a theme of the day (for example, recipes with fruits and flowers; recipes invented thinking of a particular person; recipes with rice; yellow recipes; red recipes; etc.). Children will have fun discovering others' recipes and they will learn to share and try new foods.

A small kitchen garden

Keeping a small kitchen garden is always very exciting for kids. You can give children different responsibility according to their age. A two and a half year old toddler can be quite effective in watering plants or helping

Photograph by Ezio Conti.

you plant seeds. Your older child can do more complex maintenance works. Everyone will enjoy and learn a lot by seeing plants grow and picking up their own food.

If you do not have garden space, you can do the same in your balcony. Many vegetables, herbs and even fruits can be grown in pots. Just ask the local nursery for what is available and easy to grow in your area.

Educational trips

You can plan trips to farmhouses to see how crops are grown, how a cow is milked or to have your child pick up an egg directly from the hen or an apple from its tree. Children love all this and they learn that *food is not grown in the supermarket.* They learn about nature, plants and animals. And being in nature always boosts health and appetite!

Traveling – what an occasion!

Traveling really challenges us when it comes to feeding our children, who are habitued to certain foods and may be naturally prone to refuse unfamiliar tastes. Nevertheless it can be a beautiful educational moment, an occasion to help our child accept diversity and maybe like it. If we do not force our child to eat everything at any cost, but we sweetly help him appreciate foods of unfamiliar shapes, smells and tastes, this will help him explore new cultures in all their dimensions. We may prepare him before traveling, by explaining to him what he will find and why should he try to cope and be open to new experiences. Children love being told new stories. Let's explain them—why in a particular region certain foods are eaten instead of others. They will be amazed. Maybe they will still be fussy with the new foods, but they will slowly build an openness to new experiences and a first hand knowledge of the world around them.

Chart 5
Tooth Brushing

Yes! For a child who has teeth, brushing is important. Initially you can let him observe you and play with the toothbrush (kids like to imitate). This will help him develop a habit. Later on, until he can brush effectively by himself, you should brush his teeth nicely, at least morning and evening (but it is advised to do it also after the child has had sugary food. Choose a very soft brush and gently clean from the gum towards the edge of the teeth. Always do it in this direction because brushing towards the gum might hurt the child. Toothpaste is not indispensable. If you want to use it choose one which is suitable for your child's age and teach him not to swallow it (children tend to swallow toothpaste because they like its sweet taste). For little children, choose a non-harmful, natural toothpaste. It does not matter if first teeth will 'in any case fall': oral hygiene is important to prevent cavities, which can be very painful and, if not cured, they might lead to further health complications.

Alimentary Allergies And Intolerances

What are they?

Some individuals show adverse reactions to foods which are otherwise innocuous for most people. Such reactions may include a wide variety of symptoms, affecting different systems – nervous system (for example, attention difficulties, weakness, vertigo, depression, hyperactivity, mood alterations, etc.), genito-urinary system (for example, fungal infections, recurrent urinary infections), respiratory system (for example, recurrent colds, asthma, etc.),

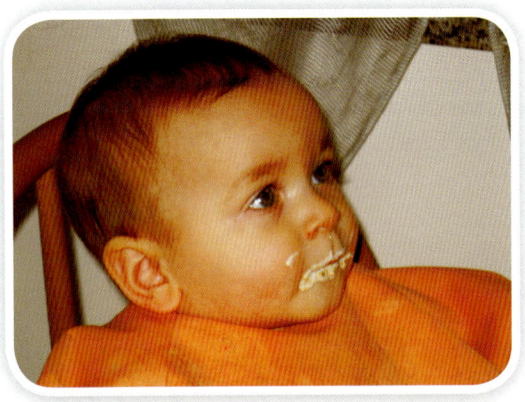

Photograph from the archive of 'In Grembo', Vercelli, Italy.

gastrointestinal system (for example, diarrhoea, vomiting, flatulence, rashes in the nappy area, etc.), heart and circulatory system, skin, bones. Other symptoms affecting the general health status of the person might be– obesity and anorexia, tonsils, gums and oral problems, and behavioural problems.

The difference between allergies and intolerances is subtle. In case of **allergy**, there is an immediate and strong reaction to the food (or rarely, the reaction happens within a few hours after the food has been consumed).

Allergies involve the person's immune system – the action of certain antibodies (IgE) causes specific molecules to release histamine, to fight the element that the body is not being able to recognize. Symptoms vary in their form and intensity, up to severe (but rare!) cases of anaphylactic shock.

In case of **intolerance**, the antibodies – IgE are not involved and the adverse reaction to the food is not immediate like in the case of allergy, it is rather slow and chronic. Symptoms of intolerance may appear upto 72 hours after the consumption of the food and are especially related to the repeated consumption of that food. This prolonged exposure of a predisposed individual causes an altered reaction of his immune system to fight the 'stranger' element. Symptoms of intolerance are normally less severe than those related to allergy, although intolerances related to enzyme deficiencies can provoke greater problems, impeding the absorption of nutrients introduced with the diet. This is for example, seen in case of coeliac disease (intolerance to gluten) or lactose intolerance (lack of lactase enzyme which is indispensable for the digestion of milk sugars). Such enzyme deficiencies may be present since birth or may slowly appear with age.

Children tend to be monotonous in their food choices. This is perhaps an ancestral instinct to prevent intoxication from unknown foods and can be respected within certain limits. However, consuming the same food every day for prolonged periods may cause adverse reactions in predisposed individuals, especially if that food contains high levels of histamine or it is a very allergenic one. That is why it is important to gently and slowly inculcate in our children the habit of a varied diet.

Alimentary Allergies And Intolerances

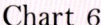

Chart 6
Some of the foods which are most likely to cause allergies and intolerances

- Cow's milk
- Fish
- Egg white
- Tomatoes
- Potatoes, eggplants, peppers
- Chocolate
- Strawberries
- Canned foods
- Pork butchery products
- Seasoned and fermented cheese
- Fermented foods and drinks

Prevention

The very first prevention towards allergies and intolerances is breastfeeding. Exclusive breastfeeding for the first six months of your child's life and prolonged breastfeeding for the first two years along with appropriate complementary foods reduce the chance of developing allergies, even in a predisposed individual. Remember that exclusive breastfeeding means that no other food other than mother's milk is given to the baby, not even water or other drinks (these are not needed if your child is successfully breastfed on demand). These are recommendations by the World Health Organization (WHO) and the best way to go about your child's nutrition. Mother's milk contains immunity factors which protect babies from infections and help their immune system to develop optimally. Cow's milk is one of the foods which is more likely to cause allergies and

EASY FIRST FOOD

intolerances because of the lactose contained in it and because the molecular chain of its proteins is very long and difficult to digest for human beings. If you or any other family member suffers from allergies, we suggest, cow's milk and formulas as first food for your baby should be avoided. If you are facing any problem with breastfeeding, you may seek competent help, like a lactation consultant or a well prepared nurse or midwife. Most breastfeeding problems can be solved with the right kind of knowledge (cases of real incapability to breastfeed are extremely rare). If at all you cannot breastfeed and you or any other relative is allergic or intolerant to cow's milk, you should find a different solution for your baby, with the help of a paediatrist. If this service is available in your area, donated mother's milk is a very good option, preferable to any kind of formula and milk substitute.

Introducing solid foods when your baby is really ready (refer – *Is your baby ready to start?*) is the second step to prevent allergies and intolerances. In case you or any other relative is allergic or intolerant to certain foods, delay the

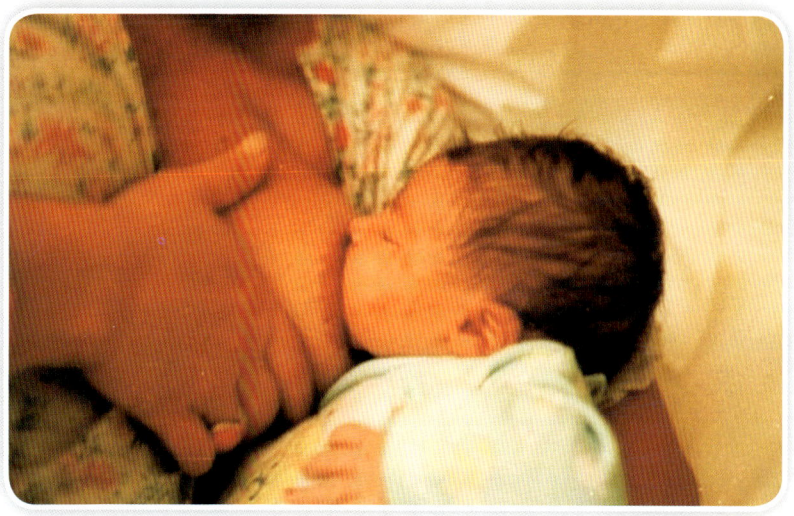

Photograph by La Leche League Italia.

introduction of those foods as much as you can. Ideally, you should wait at least one year before introducing that food. Once you have started, go about it gradually. Give the baby a small quantity of that food, observe the reaction and if no problem arises, increase the dose slowly.

A healthy, stress-free lifestyle also helps to prevent allergies and intolerances. Keep your child in open air as much as you can, avoid polluted atmospheres (pollution makes our body more sensitive to allergenic factors) but do not be obsessed with hygienic norms. Play with mud, take off your child's shoes, sometimes, in the park!

You do not need to use antibacterial soaps daily, neither on your child's skin neither on his clothes. Hand sanitizers are not meant for daily use, but for occasional circumstances. It has in fact been seen that this excessive sanitization is responsible for the increase in allergic diseases. Nowadays, apparently our immune system is less strong because of lack of exposure to pathogenic agents. It is like an athlete who lacks routine exercise and is not ready when he needs to perform. In case of allergies, we could say that our immune system acts like a football player who starts fighting his own team instead of the adversary one.

Chose fresh, seasonal fruits and vegetables – if possible, organic. Avoid junk foods and foods containing additives.

Have your child practice regular (but not excessive) physical activity, preferably in open air and in a less polluted environment. If you live in a big city, visit big parks as much as you can. Here, the air will be relatively cleaner.

Avoid stress. The family should consume meals slowly, sitting together and taking enough time, do not be in a hurry. Let the meal be a pleasant moment for your child and for yourself.

Take care of your child's intestines, by leading an active lifestyle and consuming healthy and natural homemade foods. Regular intestinal motions keep the immune system strong.

Diagnosis

Allergies and intolerances manifest themselves through a wide variety of symptoms – digestive disorders, skin disorders, irritability, sleep problems, etc. (refer to the beginning of this chapter for more details).

The first simple way to individualize an adverse reaction to a particular food is the so – called elimination diet.

If you notice signs of allergy or intolerance in your child after consuming a particular food, eliminate that food from his diet totally (beware of hidden ingredients and carefully read labels of packaged foods), for at least fifteen days. Observe your child; if the symptoms disappear, it is possible that he is allergic or intolerant to that food. Now reintroduce the food in his diet and see if the symptoms reappear. To be sure of the effectiveness of this experiment you will have to reintroduce the food in massive doses. If the symptoms reappear, the allergy/intolerance is proven. If not, you may try the same with other foods, until you find the one which is responsible for your child's problem.

In case the symptoms are severe and you are not sure of the causing agent, you can eliminate all the foods which are likely to provoke allergies / intolerances for fifteen days and if the symptoms disappear, reintroduce the foods one by one (with some days distance) until you find the culprit.

Alimentary allergies and intolerances can also be individualized by medical personnel through several tests (but they have more validity in case of allergy than intolerance). The most common tests are:

Alimentary Allergies And Intolerances

1. Blood test.
2. Skin prick test (it is painless, safe and it gives quick results; the skin is pricked with a small amount for the allergen to observe reactions – local itching and redness).
3. Food challenge (it is most accurate for alimentary allergies and it is done by administering the patient an increasingly higher dose of the allergenic food and monitoring the reaction).

What to do in case of proven allergy or intolerance?

In case of a proven allergy or intolerance, that particular food should be avoided. Beware of hidden ingredients (for example, eggs or milk contained in bakery products, glutamate – made from wheat gluten – contained in taste improvers and other processed items).

When buying packaged foods, always read labels carefully to be sure that the product does not contain the food that needs to be avoided, or it has been produced in a factory where that food is processed.

Mild intolerances may disappear with growth, when your child's digestive system becomes more mature and functional. After avoiding contact with the food that causes the intolerance for a sufficient stretch of time, you may slowly try to reintroduce it in your child's diet and observe the reaction.

Although, allergies might disappear after avoiding contact with the allergenic factor for a certain amount of time and improving one's general lifestyle, you still may need to be more careful, especially if the allergy is severe. Do not try self-made experiments; but always act under medical advice and supervision.

EASY FIRST FOOD

Alimentary Allergies And Intolerances

PART–II

Recipes From the World- To Be Made For and With Your Child

Recipes From the World-To Be Made For and With Your Child

Vegetable clear soup

Serves 1-2 people

Ingredients

1 cup seasonal vegetables, chopped

4 cups water

1-2 pinches salt

Method

1. Place the ingredients in a boiling pan of your choice.
2. Boil everything until the water becomes half its original volume.
3. Remove or strain the vegetables through a sieve and serve.

Note

1. *It can be used as a base to prepare several dishes, to cook cereals and pulses and as the first way to introduce small children to vegetables.*
2. *For a non-vegetarian soup, small pieces of chicken can be*

Rice cream

Serves 1 child

Ingredients

3 spoons brown rice

2-3 cups water or clear soup

Method

1. Boil brown rice in either water or clear soup on a low fire until the rice is very soft and breaks easily if mashed with a fork.
2. Add water or clear soup until needed.
3. Mash or grind.

Note

1. It is ideal for the introduction of first cereal.
2. It can be the base of several preparations.
3. You may add mashed boiled vegetables, meat, lentils or mashed seasonal fruits to it.

Rice and fruit pudding

Serves 3-4

Ingredients

1 cup brown rice

6 cups water

1 chopped apple

1 chopped pear

1 spoon raisins or dates (finely chopped)

Method

1. Boil the rice and the dry fruits in the water at a very low flame until the water is almost totally absorbed and

the rice is very soft.
2. Add the fruits and cook for another 5-10 minutes.
3. Stir and mash if the child is very small.
4. Serve hot or place in pudding moulds and let it cool in the fridge.

Apple treat

Serves 4

Ingredients

8 apples

2 teaspoon raisins or dates (finely chopped)

Ground cinnamon according to taste

2 glasses water

Method

1. Place the ingredients in a boiling pan.
2. Cover and let them simmer on very low fire until the apples mash and the water is absorbed.
3. Mash with a fork and add cinnamon according to your taste.
4. It can be served warm or cold.

Note

It is very useful in case of constipation.

Pumpkin risotto

Serves 3-4

Ingredients

2 cups pumpkin, cut into cubes

EASY FIRST FOOD

1 cup rice (better to use short grain or risotto type)

1 chopped onion

1 teaspoon or a small branch of rosemary

3-4 cups clear soup

3 spoons olive oil

Salt according to taste

1 teaspoon butter or grated parmesan cheese

Method

1. Heat the oil in a large pan (like a wok or a wide frying pan).
2. Add onion and rosemary. Cook on gentle fire until golden.
3. Add the pumpkin. Cook for 5 minutes and add the rice.
4. Roast it until golden and add tepid clear soup slowly, on low fire, until the rice is cooked. Stir frequently.

Photograph by Amoli Kaur.

Recipes From the World-To Be Made For and With Your Child

5. You may add a teaspoon of butter and / or parmesan cheese at the end of the preparation.

Sesame flowers

Serves 3-4

Ingredients

1 big-medium size cauliflower

1 big-medium size broccoli flower

2 teaspoons sesame

2 teaspoons olive oil

1 cup natural white yoghurt

2 pinches salt

Method

1. Steam cauliflower and broccoli taking care not to overcook them. They should maintain their live white and green colour; they should not become too soft in order to preserve their properties and be appreciated by children. Kids might not like them when overcooked because their smell becomes very strong and their taste changes.

2. Separate the branches in order to obtain several little flowers. Place the flowers nicely in a dish and let them cool.

3. Roast the sesame seeds in a pan until they become light brown and keep aside.

4. Beat the yoghurt with the oil and the salt. Sprinkle on the flowers.

5. Sprinkle the sesame seeds on top and serve.

Green rice cake

Serves 3-4

Ingredients

1 cup boiled brown rice

1 cup steamed and chopped spinach

1 chopped onion

1 cup mashed cottage cheese

3 eggs

1 pinch pepper

Salt according to taste

2 teaspoons olive oil or any other oil procured by mechanical extraction

Method

1. Roast the onion in the oil, in a large frying pan.
2. Add rice and spinach. Roast them for another 2-3 minutes.

Recipes From the World-To Be Made For and With Your Child

3. Add the eggs, after beating them with salt, pepper and cottage cheese.
4. Cover and cook both sides on low fire.

Ravioli

Serves 3-4

Ingredients

For the dough

1 and 1/2 cup whole wheat flour

1 and 1/2 cup white flour

Water for kneading the dough

For the filling

250 grams cottage cheese

1 cup steamed spinach

1 teaspoon salt

1 pinch pepper

1/2 teaspoon coriander powder

For garnishing

Butter or olive oil or fresh tomato sauce

Method

For the dough

1. Prepare the dough mixing the two kinds of flour. Add water very slowly, working the dough with your hand until it becomes elastic and compact, but dry. The dough is ready when it feels like plastiline, it can be easily worked without sticking to your hands. For this purpose, add water very slowly and in small quantities. In case, excessive water falls in the mixture, you can correct the preparation by adding more flour.
2. Keep the dough aside in a bowl.

For the filling

1. Crush and mix together cheese and spinach.
2. Add salt, pepper and coriander powder.

For making Ravioli

1. Roll the dough with a roller until it becomes approximately 1-2 millimetres thin. Cut it into squares or triangles (approximately 3-4 cms per side).
2. Place a small amount of the filling on a square or triangle and close it with another one on top, so that you have a series of stuffed triangles or squares. Let them dry on a clean surface covered with flour, and sprinkle flour on top.
3. Boil the ravioli in abundant salty water for approximately 10 minutes or until the texture feels slightly soft.
4. Drain them and serve with butter or olive oil or a homemade tomato sauce.

Note

It is a complete meal; to be offered after the child is one year old.

Recipes From the World-To Be Made For and With Your Child

Tomato sauce

Ingredients

Fresh well ripened tomatoes
Water for boiling tomatoes
Salt according to taste
Garlic
Basil according to taste
Olive oil

Method

1. Boil abundant water.
2. After putting off the fire, put the tomatoes in the water and leave them for 10-15 minutes. Take them out of the water, peel them and chop them.
3. In a pan, warm the olive oil with garlic and add the tomatoes after the garlic starts spreading its smell.
4. Let the tomatoes cook on low fire until they become like a puree and their colour is warmer.
5. Add salt and freshly crushed basil according to your taste.

Pizza

Serves 4

Ingredients

500 grams white flour
1 teaspoon salt
4 teaspoons olive oil
30 grams yeast
1 and 1/2 cups water

1 pinch sugar

1 cup tomato sauce

1 cup grated or chopped mozzarella cheese

Method

1. Melt the yeast in half cup slightly tepid water, with a pinch of sugar. The water should not be too warm, otherwise the yeast will die. Let it rest for five minutes so that it becomes active.

2. Pour the yeast with its water in a large bowl and add the remaining water.

3. Gradually add the flour, beating the mixture with a fork, until the thickness of the mixture will not allow you to easily work it with the fork.

4. Add the salt, the oil and the remaining flour, working it energetically with your hands until it becomes a soft but compact dough. The dough should not be sticky, so you may adjust the quantity of flour and water accordingly. Small variations in the water/flour proportion will not harm the result. Just keep in mind that the dough should feel soft like plastiline and not sticky.

5. Let the dough rest for at least one hour, covered with a cloth, far from currents. The ideal place is the oven, preheated at 50°C. Put if off before introducing the dough.

6. Once the dough has risen enough, work it again with your hands for a couple of minutes and spread it with your finger tips in a baking tray oiled with olive oil. Make it approximately half a cm tall and spread tomato sauce on top.

7. Bake it at high temperature (approximately 250°C). The time required for cooking varies according to the oven.

To check whether the pizza is cooked, pinch the pizza with a fork. If you see that the fork comes out dry, sprinkle mozzarella cheese on top.

8. Let it bake for another 2-5 minutes and remove from the oven.

Note

You may add grilled vegetables of your choice and /or oregano or basil as topping.

Oatmeal 'omelette'

Serves 3-4

Ingredients

3 cups oatmeal

Water to soak the oatmeal

1 cup chopped vegetables of your choice (for example, zucchini)

1 chopped onion

Salt according to taste

Pepper according to taste

Oil procured from mechanical extraction

Method

1. Pour the oatmeal in a bowl and cover with water. Mix and keep in the fridge for 2 hours. Add salt and pepper according to your taste.

2. In a large frying pan, heat a veil of oil and cook the onions and the vegetable until the chosen vegetable is ready.

3. Add the oatmeal preparation, cover and cook at very low fire on both sides, until the omelette is crispy and golden.

Crispy soy nuggets

Serves 3-4

Ingredients

2 cups soy nuggets

Water

Salt according to taste

Garlic

Rosemary

Sage

1 lemon or orange

Oil procured from mechanical extraction

For serving

Sliced tomatoes

Lettuce

Natural yoghurt

Pita bread

Recipes From the World-To Be Made For and With Your Child

Method

1. Boil a big quantity of water. Put off the fire after the water has boiled and put the soy nuggets in the water.
2. Let them rest for 5-10 minutes. Remove them from the water, rinse and squeeze out all the water they have absorbed.
3. Heat a small quantity of oil in a frying pan or in a wok.
4. Add garlic, rosemary, sage and finally the nuggets. Add salt and cook on low fire, without covering, until the nuggets are brown and crispy.
5. Stir frequently.
6. Add lemon or orange juice and cook for another 2-3 minutes, stirring, on high flame.
7. Serve with natural yoghurt, lettuce, raw tomatoes and pita bread.

Baked felafels

Serves 3-4

Ingredients

1 cup dried grams

1/4 cup flour

1 chopped onion

1/3 cup fresh chopped coriander

1 teaspoon cumin

1 teaspoon dry coriander leaves or seeds

1 chopped garlic clove

Salt according to taste

Photograph by Ezio Conti.

EASY FIRST FOOD

Olive oil or any other oil procured from mechanical extraction

For garnishing

Fresh cut vegetables and natural yoghurt

Method

1. Boil the grams, after soaking overnight.
2. Drain the water from them. Mash them and add the other ingredients.
3. Mix everything carefully and form small balls with the preparation.
4. Flatten the balls and place them in a baking pan where you have previously spread a light veil of oil.
5. Bake at 180°, stirring frequently, until both sides are golden brown.
6. Serve with fresh cut vegetables and natural yoghurt.

Potato gnocchi

Serves 4

Ingredients

1 kg potatoes

300 grams flour

1 egg

Salt according to taste

Photograph by Franca Giovagnini.

Method

1. Boil the potatoes, then peel and mash them.
2. Add the other ingredients and work into a soft and even dough.
3. Pick up a small amount of preparation and work it

with your hands as if it was plastiline, to form a 1 cm tall 'snake.' Cut the snake into 1 cm long pieces. Go on until you are done with the entire dough.

4. Now you may leave the gnocchi like this or give them the traditional curly shape by rolling them gently on a fork.
5. Boil in abundant salty water until they come on the water surface. As they reach the water surface, quickly take them out with a strainer ladle.
6. Garnish with olive oil or tomato sauce or any other sauce of your liking.

Avocado sauce

Ingredients

1 ripe avocado

Juice of 1 lime

1-2 pinches salt

1 pinch pepper

1 teaspoon olive oil

Method

1. Mash the avocado with a fork.
2. Add the other ingredients, and keep mashing until it becomes a cream. Avoid pepper for smaller children.

Mini veggy cakes

Makes approximately 12 cakes

Ingredients

4 eggs

1 cup steamed spinach

EASY FIRST FOOD

Photograph by Ezio Conti.

1 cup steamed mixed vegetables, cut in small pieces (for example, carrots, French beans, asparagus, etc.)

1 cup mashed potatoes

1 cup grated parmesan (alternately you can use mashed cottage cheese)

Salt according to taste

Method

1. Separate the egg whites from the yolk. Beat the yolks and the whites separately until they become foam.
2. Mix them together and add the parmesan. Distribute the mixture equally into three bowls.
3. Add a different vegetable preparation in each bowl (for example, spinach in one, potatoes in the other and mixed veggies in the last).
4. Mix each of them and pour in muffin moulds.
5. Bake at a temperature of approximately 180°C. To check if the cakes are done, pierce them with a fork or toothpick. If it comes out dry, they are ready.

Peanut butter

Ingredients

2 cups unsalted peanuts

1-2 teaspoons peanut oil

Sugar according to taste

Salt according to taste

Method

1. Roast the peanuts until golden and grind them while they are still warm.
2. Add the oil to soften the paste and easily turn it into a cream.
3. Consume natural or add sugar and salt according to your taste.

Vegetarian paella

Serves 4-6

Ingredients

2 cups rice

1 cup boiled gram

1 cup fresh green peas

2-3 sliced peppers (red, yellow or green)

2 cups French beans

1 aubergine, cut into cubes

1-2 chopped tomatoes

1 large chopped onion

2-3 garlic cloves

1/2 teaspoon saffron

EASY FIRST FOOD

Salt according to taste

Olive oil

Water for cooking rice

Paprika (additional)

Fresh parsley (additional)

Method

1. Infuse the saffron for a few minutes in a small quantity of tepid water.

2. In a large wok, heat a veil of oil and cook the onion and garlic cloves on a low fire, stirring frequently, until they become soft and golden.

Photograph by Ezio Conti

3. Add the saffron, the paprika (if you like it), tomatoes, grams, peas and French beans. Cook for 2 minutes.

4. Now add the rice and stir frequently for another 2 minutes.

5. Add warm water and salt. Cover the pan and let the rice cook on a low flame until ready.

6. Meanwhile, stir fry the aubergine cubes and the sliced peppers (separately) until soft. Do not cover the pan during this operation. Keep stirring frequently.

7. Keep aside and mix with the rice once everything is ready.

8. You may finally sprinkle chopped parsley on top of the dish.

Recipes From the World-To Be Made For and With Your Child

Hummus
Ingredients
250 grams boiled gram

1 garlic clove

1 teaspoon tahine paste (sesame paste)

Juice of 1 sweet lime

Salt according to taste

Water (or the cooking water of grams)

Method
1. Grind all the ingredients together, adding enough water to make a soft spreadable cream.
2. Serve with pita bread or fresh raw vegetables.

Sesame sweets
Serves 4-6

Ingredients
1 cup of sesame seeds

1 cup brown sugar

2 teaspoons butter or clarified butter

Method
1. Roast the sesame seeds in a non-stick pan, stirring continuously with a wooden spoon, until golden brown.
2. Remove from the fire and keep aside.
3. Melt the sugar in the same pan. Add the butter and the sesame seeds. Keep stirring until the ingredients are evenly mixed together.
4. Place the mixture on a wet ceramic or steel plate and give it a flat shape, using a wet spoon or wet hands.
5. Let it cool and cut into pieces.

EASY FIRST FOOD

Gram flour pizzas

Serves 1

Ingredients

3 teaspoons gram flour

1 pinch salt

2 teaspoons tomato sauce

1/2 cup mozzarella cubes

1 spoon cooking oil

Water

Method

1. Mix the gram flour with a small quantity of water, adding the water slowly until the mixture has the thickness of a beaten egg.
2. Add salt and cook on both sides in a frying pan, as if it was an omelette, after heating the oil.
3. When both sides are golden brown, lower the fire to

minimum. Quickly spread the tomato sauce on top, sprinkle mozzarella cheese and cover.

4. Put off the fire and let it remain covered until the mozzarella cheese has melted.

Bottle gourd pizzas
Serves 3-4

Ingredients
2 bottle gourds, not too big

Tomato sauce

Mozzarella cheese

Salt according to taste

Oil procured from mechanical extraction

Method
1. Slice the bottle gourds (approximately 1/2 cm thin), grill them and add salt.

2. Place the slices on a large frying pan, covered with a veil of oil.
3. Spread each slice with tomato sauce and add small pieces of mozzarella cheese on top.
4. Cover and cook at very low flame until the mozzarella melts.

Note
The same dish can be prepared with aubergines or other vegetables of your choice (for example, aubergines or zucchini).

Pumpkin fantasy

Ingredients
Pumpkin

Salt according to taste

Oil procured from mechanical extraction

Boiled rice

Cottage cheese

Flour

Method

1. Slice the pumpkin (it should be approximately 5mm thin). Place them in a baking pan or on a frying pan, after covering it with a veil of oil. Add salt and cook on both sides until soft inside and slightly crispy on the surface. You may bake it or cook on slow fire. For a lighter version you may steam the slices, taking care that you do not break them.
2. Let them cool a bit and cut into funny shapes using biscuits moulds. Keep the shapes aside.
3. Mash the leftovers of this cutting procedure and mix with cottage cheese, salt and boiled rice.

4. Form small compact balls out of this mixture. Roll them in a veil of flour and bake or cook until crispy on the surface.

5. Place the balls on a serving dish with the pumpkin shapes that you have kept aside.

Mini sticks

Ingredients

Food leftovers

Cheese

Tomatoes

Raw vegetables cut in pieces

Olives

Anything, according to your taste and what you have at home

(you may use boiled eggs or small pieces of omelette, ham, chicken, even fruits)

Toothpicks

Photograph by Ezio Conti

Method

Use your creativity. Stick the ingredients on the toothpicks to form pleasant compositions and colour combinations. Kids will love them, and they will love to prepare them as well.

Rainbow yogurt

Serves 4-6

Ingredients

3 cups natural white yoghurt

1 cup chopped or ground nuts (for example, almonds,

walnuts, peanuts, etc.)

1 teaspoon honey

4 cups seasonal fruits of two different colours (2+2)

Method

1. In a bowl, mix the yoghurt with nuts and honey and keep aside.
2. Grind the chosen fruits separately, so that you have two mixtures of different colours.
3. In glasses or transparent pudding moulds, pour different coloured layers of the three mixtures (one colour fruit, then yoghurt, then the other fruit, then yoghurt and again…).

Note

You may add chopped biscuits, cornflakes, raisins or muesli to the composition.

French pancakes (crèpes)

Makes 3-4 small crèpes

Ingredients

1 egg

2 teaspoons brown sugar (for sweet pancakes) or

2 pinches salt (for salty pancakes)

2 teaspoons flour

Milk

1 teaspoon butter

For the filling

1. For sweet pancakes, you can use jam, honey, fruit,

Recipes From the World-To Be Made For and With Your Child

chocolate spread, brown sugar and lemon or anything according to your taste.

2. For salty pancakes, try cottage cheese or mozzarella cheese, spinach, mushrooms or any other vegetable or a combination of vegetables and cheese.

For the pancakes

1. In a bowl, beat the egg with flour and sugar or salt, adding milk slowly, until the mixture has the consistency of beaten eggs. It should neither be too thick nor too liquid; if you let a bit of the mixture fall down from the spoon, it should feel just slightly sticky and make a sort of 'wire.'

2. Heat a teaspoon of butter in a small frying pan (about 20 cm in diameter).

3. Pour a thin veil of the mixture (approximately 1-2 mm thick). Cover and cook on both sides until golden brown, taking care that the pancake does not break while stirring.

4. Remove from fire, spread the chosen sweet or salty mixture and fold it in half. Serve warm.

Almond cake

Ingredients

300 grams almonds

100 grams butter

100 grams dark chocolate

100 grams brown sugar

3 eggs

White sugar and/or almonds to decorate

Photograph by Ezio Conti

Method

1. Grind the almonds.
2. Heat butter and chocolate, separately, until they melt. Do not put them on direct flame; put in a small pan placed on bigger pan filled with three fingers of water. While doing this, make sure that the water does not reach the contents of the inner pan.
3. Mix all the ingredients and place them in a cake mould, after spreading butter on it.
4. Bake at 180°C until it makes a crust. Note that this cake should remain soft and slightly wet inside.
5. After cooling, you may decorate the cake with ground white sugar or ground/whole almonds.

Biscuits

Ingredients

150 grams whole wheat flour

150 grams maize flour

150 grams butter

100 grams brown sugar

2 eggs

Method

1. Leave the butter out of the fridge until soft. Cut it in small pieces and mix it with the flours using your fingertips. Do not make it compact, but leave it friable.
2. Add 1 full egg, 1 egg white, sugar, and mix. This time you will want the mixture to become a compact dough.
3. Slowly add milk, in small quantity, until, while mixing energetically with your hands, the dough becomes firm and elastic, not wet, like plastiline.

4. Roll the dough with a roller until it is approximately 4-5 cm thin. Cut it in shapes, as you like. You may use a biscuit cutter or simply a round glass.

5. Heat the oven at 150-180°C and bake for 10-15 minutes. Mind that ovens are different from each other, so you might need to vary timings and temperature accordingly. The biscuits are ready when they become golden brown. Even if they are soft you can remove them from the oven. They will become hard while cooling.

Note

To make 'richer' biscuits, you may add crushed nuts and / or raisins to the ready dough, mixing them before cutting the shapes.

Yoghurt and fruit ice creams

Makes 6-8 ice creams

Ingredients

200 grams full cream natural yoghurt

2 ripe bananas

1 cup chopped seasonal fruits

Method

1. Grind everything together and pour in ice cream moulds (preferably those with a stick, to make lollies).

2. Let the ice creams freeze and then let the kids enjoy. My kids simply love them and they are made of healthy ingredients, without added sugar. This is a smart strategy to make fussy little mouths accept fruits. You may also increase the quantity of fruit and reduce the quantity of yogurt. The result will just be slightly more icy and less creamy. I found the bananas very important to give sweetness and texture to the preparation.

Semolina cake

Ingredients

1 cup semolina

1 litre milk

1/2 cup sugar

1/3 cup raisins

1 spoon unsalted butter

Method

1. Bring the milk to a boil then remove it from the fire and gradually add the semolina, stirring quickly to avoid formation of knots.
2. Put back on low fire and stir continuously, until the mixture is thick and cooked.
3. Remove from fire, add raisins and sugar, and mix.
4. You may now bake it or not. Baking will just serve to make a slightly crispy crust and to give more solidity to the sweet.
5. Butter a baking pan, pour the semolina and bake at 180°C for a short time, until the surface becomes golden.
6. Remove from the oven. Once cool keep it in the fridge.
7. Cut into cubes and serve cold.

Note

If you choose not to bake the cake, just pour the mixture in a large flat container (keep in mind that the cake should be approximately 3-4 cm tall) and cool in the fridge. Once it is solid, cut into cubes and serve.

Recipes From the World-To Be Made For and With Your Child

Chocolate almonds

Ingredients

1 cup almonds

1/2 cup brown sugar

3-4 teaspoons cocoa powder

Method

1. Spread the cocoa powder on a large plate and keep aside.
2. Heat the sugar in a frying pan until it melts into caramel. Add the almonds and stir until they are all covered with caramel.
3. Remove the almonds from the fire and roll them in the cocoa powder. Separate them if they stick together.
4. Serve tepid.

Note

Very good in winters and in case of mental fatigue.

Refreshing mint water

Ingredients

1 and 1/2 litre water

1 bunch fresh sweet mint

1/2 glass brown sugar

Bring the water to boil. Add the mint and the sugar. Boil for 5 minutes. Serve cool, garnished with a sprig of mint and a lemon slice.

Photograph by Ezio Conti

EASY FIRST FOOD

Bibliography

Balaskas J., *Naturalmente mamma*, Pisani, 2004.

Binagli I., Pincini F., *Intolleranze zero!*, Tecniche nuove, 2008.

Bondil A., Kaplan M., *Alimentazione in gravidanza e nella prima infanzia secondo il metodo Kousmine*, Tecniche nuove, 1991.

Bumgarner N.J., *Mothering your nursing toddler*, LLLI, 2000.

Capo A., *Curarsi con frutta e verdura*, Orsa Maggiore, 1995.

Carlos Gonzales, *Il mio bambino non mi mangia. Consigli per prevenire e risolvere il problema*, Bonomi, 2003.

Del Pup L., *Alimentazione in gravidanza e allattamento. Consigli pratici per la salute e il benessere della madre e del bambino*, Editeam, 2006.

La Leche League Italia, *Svezzamento, passo dopo passo*, La Leche League Italia, 2002.

La Leche League International, *L'arte dell'allattamento materno*, LLLI, 2005.

Lepetit de la Bigne G., Amante A., *L'alimentazione vegetariana*, Tecniche Nuove, 1990.

Trapani G., *Bambini a tavola. La giusta alimentazione per crescere sani e forti*, Salute e Natura, 2005.

Sears W. and Sears M., *The Baby Book. Everything you need to know about your baby from birth to age two*, Thorsons, 2005.

Valpiana T., *L'alimentazione naturale del bambino. Allattamento, svezzamento, ricette salutari fino ai 6 anni*, Red, 1998.

Valpiana T., Parona M., *Le ricette per l'alimentazione naturale del bambino. Pranzi e merendine: Tante idee gustose dallo svezzamento ai 10 anni*, Red, 1999.